The Communion of the Holy Spirit

*Ancient Spirituality for the Kingdom:
A Contemporary Portrait of the Fifty Homilies of Saint
Macarius the Egyptian*

The Communion of the Holy Spirit

Ancient Spirituality for the Kingdom:

A Contemporary Portrait of the Fifty Homilies of Saint Macarius the Egyptian

Book 1

Professor George Tadros, M.D.

AGORA
UNIVERSITY
PRESS

The Communion of the Holy Spirit
Ancient Spirituality for the Kingdom: A Contemporary Portrait of
the Fifty Homilies of Saint Macarius the Egyptian

Copyright © 2020 by Agora University Press

All rights reserved. Printed in the United States of America. No part of this
book may be used or reproduced in any manner whatsoever without written
permission except in the case of brief quotations embodied in critical articles or
reviews.

For information contact : aupress@aui.ac
Agora University Press http://www.aui.ac

ISBN 978-1-950831-11-1

HIS HOLINESS POPE TAWADROS II
*118th Pope and Patriarch of the great city of
Alexandria and the See of St. Mark.*

HIS HOLINESS PATRIARCH IGNATIUS
APHREM II
Patriarch of Antioch and All the East

This work is dedicated to those who love God with their entire being and desire to know Him more as they prepare themselves for a journey into the depths of His love.

Contents

Acknowledgments i
Foreword iv
Preface 1
  1. Saint Macarius of Egypt 5
  2. Prepare Your Soul to be Christ's Throne 13
  3. New Clothes for the New Man 26
  4. Into the Image of Him Who Died for Us 32
  5. A New Creation 47
  6. Harmony Between the Holy Spirit and Our Free Will 60
  7. Our Unity with the Holy Spirit 67
  8. The Seal 71
  9. Illumination for the Eyes of Our Hearts 83
  10. A Personal Invitation to the Kingdom 88
  11. The Anointing 100
  12. True Richness 110
  13. Be Filled with the Holy Spirit 117
  14. Adornment of the Spirit 124
  15. External and Internal Spiritual Warfare 130
  16. Victory in Spiritual Warfare 135
  17. The Yeast 138
  18. Honor of Unity 143
  19. Know Yourself 162
  20. Birth from Above 178
  21. Glorious Resurrection 186
  22. True Christians 195
  23. The Purpose of Divine Scriptures 200
  24. Put Off the Old Man 202
  25. The Indwelling of the Holy Spirit 205
  26. The Treasure of the Spirit in Clay Vessels 209
Conclusion 213
Bibliography 258
About the Author 260

Acknowledgments

In my continuously busy professional life with long working days and endless competing tasks, engrossing myself in Saint Macarius' teaching and rewriting his homilies in a new style gave me great pleasure and maintained my psychological balance at work and home. But it also took away a lot of time that I could have spent with my wife and daughters. Therefore, I am forever indebted to my wonderful wife, Nermyne Tadros, who supported me for better and for worse since the first day we met and throughout my life journey, professional career, and bringing up our children. She regularly advised me on this book while continuously sacrificing many of our family commitments and activities to allow this book to reach your hands. I am also grateful to my two daughters, Maria and Agiya, who gave me a youthful perspective on the cultural changes and modern choice of words, and indeed, their views on gender equality. Moreover, they reviewed the first draft and gave their critique alongside their endless encouragement and support.

I would love to register the support and love I received from Anba Epiphanius of Saint Macarius monastery who agreed to meet me at short notice, discussed the idea of this book, and generously gave me all his spiritual and intellectual support to complete this work. His Grace kindly planned to forward this book, but was sadly taken from among us by murderous hands before this book was ready for publication. I pray that his prayers will be acceptable intercessions for us in front of the throne of Christ. I cannot even describe the depth of my gratitude to Father Younan El-Makary who, despite the great distance, technological challenges, and communication barriers, kindly agreed to review the book against the original text. His thorough review was of a superb quality that reflected his serious scholastic approach and his deep love of Saint Macarius' teaching. He frequently gave me advice on many spiritual concepts, biblical references, and the use of words and phrases using Greek, Coptic, Latin, French, and English texts in an extremely thorough manner to make sure that what is conveyed in this book truly reflects Saint Macarius' teaching despite the change of writing style. His work was essential to the production of this book and very valuable.

I am deeply indebted to Virgil Tabry and my other reviewer who edited many parts of the manuscript and gave unfailing support, investing plenty of time to thoroughly review every word and every phrase, and made significant contributions that shaped this book.

I am grateful to my dear Bishop Anba Missael of Birmingham, England, who always taught me the real meaning of love, humility, and choosing the last seat. Also, I am thankful to Father Youhanna Yani who guided me to serve non-Arabic speaking communities with love and dedication. I am very grateful to Father Peter El-Sobky who gave me many resources to serve and never complained when I demanded more, which he always gave graciously. I would like to express my appreciation to Father Mark Aziz who continuously supported me and was always available to give me an instant supply of Biblical references.

I am honored that Bishop David of New York and New England, kindly agreed to foreword this book despite his very busy schedule. His Grace gave me much valuable advice and reviewed the final manuscript. I have known Anba David since he served as a monk in Saint Mary and Saint Mark's Coptic Orthodox Centre in the Midlands. He was always very caring, loving, and wise and a great support to the ministry of God.

George Tadros

The Assumption of Saint Mary
22nd August 2020 AD
16th Mesore 1736 AM

Foreword

I am delighted to congratulate Doctor George Tadros on the completion of this prominent literary work examining the Orthodox Christian understanding of monasticism through the life and sayings of one of the great Coptic monks, Saint Macarius the Great. Dr. Tadros' thoughtful writing presents this holy life of consecration in a light that fully captures its great significance within our Church, and will undoubtedly be appreciated by readers--old and young--who may seek a more fulfilling life through a journey of asceticism and contemplation. Believed to be the birthplace of monasticism, the deserts of Egypt have gifted the world with spiritual greats like Saint Anthony the Great, recognized as the father of monasticism throughout the world, and the father of monks in Egypt. Having answered a calling at the age of twenty to forsake everything and follow the Lord into the desert, Saint Anthony dedicated the remainder of his life to the pursuit of perfection through asceticism and prayer. On many occasions, he endured spiritual and physical afflictions from the devil, which led him even further into the desert and deepened his relationship with Christ. Eventually, the Lord brought to light his struggles, allowing for discipleship and the establishment of this spiritual lifestyle of complete consecration to the Lord.

Among Saint Anthony's most notable disciples, Saint Macarius the Great also made a lasting impact on the understanding and establishment of monastic life. During his days in the Nitrian desert learning from Saint Anthony, Saint Macarius developed a deep understanding of the monastic lifestyle and took to writing as a means of recording and sharing what he learned. He established monastic communities throughout the desert of Scetis and discipled thousands of monks, including many notable ascetics such as Saint Arsenius, the brothers Saints Maximus and Domadius, and others who went on to continue the ascetic tradition and train their own disciples. As you will note, Dr. Tadros writes in a contemporary fashion that has made ancient writings and practices accessible to today's readers. Among the many treasures of this book, Dr. Tadros presents a translation of Saint Macarius' teachings and instructions in a manner that is easily comprehendible and relatable to the modern-day reader. In addition to the insight he offers into monastic asceticism, this work includes prayers that the reader may contemplate on as he or she learns more about the profound benefits of the austere lifestyle pursued by many throughout the history of the Church.

Dr. Tadros' focus on the various writings of the great desert fathers touches upon several important aspects of our spiritual development and addresses topics that are relevant to the life and journey of every Christian. Through his analysis, we come to learn that a theologian develops not through academic endeavors and ceaseless study, but through a life of prayer that leads to an intense personal relationship with God, and unlocks the mysteries of the divine nature. This work likewise addresses core Orthodox theological concepts, including the Orthodox understanding of Original Sin, the subsequent corruption of human nature, and an authentic understanding of Deification as discussed by Saint Athanasius. Simply speaking, Dr. Tadros took the time-tested monastic teachings and instructions of Saint Macarius the Great, one of the most influential desert fathers, and expressed them in a contemporary written form appealing to readers of all ages.

I commend Dr. Tadros on this tremendous and valuable undertaking, and look forward to the next book in this series. I pray that this book becomes a source of blessing to all of its readers through the intercession of our Heavenly Mother, the Holy Theotokos Saint Mary, the prayers of Saint Macarius the Great and all the saints, as well as the prayers and support of our blessed father His Holiness Pope Tawadros II. Amen.

Bishop Anba David
Coptic Orthodox Diocese of New York and New England

7th August 2020 AD
1st Mesore 1736 AM

Preface

By the grace of our Lord and the guidance of the Holy Spirit, and after years of reluctance, I have started this journey to present to our fellow Christians from all age groups and all backgrounds the thought and teaching of Saint Macarius the Egyptian, who is also known as Macarius the Great. Most Copts call him Abu Makar el-Kibeer or Anba Makar. Though his teaching is very Orthodox and authentic, his homilies have influenced Pietist groups ranging from the spiritual Franciscans (in the church of the Western Roman Empire) to Eastern Orthodox monastic groups. He also influenced modern Western teachers such as John Wesley (the founder of the Methodist Church) who used his homilies in many of his sermons and songs (Tharwat Maher Nagib, Cairo, 2010). I personally found his writing full of grace that rekindles our love for God very easily in a disarming manner. Moreover, I found it all grounded in a deep understanding of the Bible that opens our hearts to explore the Bible in more depth.

The fifty homilies were accredited to Macarius throughout the ages until some modern scholars, in the twentieth century, such as L. Villecourt (1920) and G. L. Marriott (1921) started shedding some doubt on the belief that Macarius was the original writer. However, A. J. Mason (Aeterna Press, 1921) gave strong evidence to prove that these fifty homilies were written by Macarius himself. Moreover, the cultural connotations used to illustrate some of his thoughts have clear Coptic connections that are easily identified by the Copts—as well as the verbal traditions, inherited literature and continuous practices among the Egyptian monks that, since the fourth century support the belief that these fifty homilies were written by Macarius himself. They were first published in Paris in 1559 by Morel, and a Latin translation appeared in 1699 and an early English translation appeared as early as 1721 followed by a few other translations. One of the most popular translations was by Mason. However, all of them seem to fail to genuinely convey the spirit of Macarius' teaching in an easily readable form, as the style of his writing belongs to the fourth century. Also, old fashioned English and culturally orientated examples are used that need to be adjusted for other cultures.

Macarius gives many illustrations to highlight our Lord's desire for our salvation and his many ways of reaching out to us. These are based fully on his deep knowledge and personal experience of the Bible which completely shaped the way he lived. His thoughts are very wide ranging, fit to be adopted by other cultures and are still exceptionally relevant for us in this modern age. However the language of the homilies has been a serious barrier even although translations have been available. This book you have in your hands is not a direct or full translation of Macarius' teaching but rather an abridgement, and it contains only twenty five of his fifty homilies. All the paragraphs have been rewritten in a more modern style with gender inclusiveness and culture neutrality. Some paragraphs have been moved across to maintain the thread of thoughts, and others were omitted or shortened when appropriate to avoid repetition, but the original paragraph numbers have been kept (not in serial order) for easy reference in case the reader wishes to examine the original text. Many Biblical verses and references were added in a style that makes it look like they were part of the manuscript, and also his original Biblical references were kept in most of the time. I have tried my best to present his teachings honestly, not as a direct translation but rather through my own reading of them. Therefore, the reader should be careful not to fully accept this script as the direct translation of Macarius' teaching. Some thoughts and prayers which are taken from the Psalms and Church fathers have been added in italics at the end of some sections to encourage a prayerful reading.

The fifty homilies of Macarius have been divided into two books; each book is based on a theme rather than on the simple order of the homilies. This book you have is Book 1, and deals with our relationship with the Holy Spirit as reflected in the title of the book. I hope this will offer easy access to the homilies and make them easily digested and readily remembered. The rest of his fifty homilies will appear in Book 2 sometime in the near future.

I hope this book will attract many English-speaking people from various cultures and backgrounds, to help people to know the Lord in a much deeper way and that our eyes may be opened to see His ways and our heart to see His love so that we can be fully united with Him in our quest for righteousness. For those who would like to search for a direct translation of Macarius' original teaching, I would recommend the full English translation of the "Fifty Spiritual Homilies of Saint Macarius The Egyptian", by A. J. Mason (1921), or the work of Father George Maloney (1992), despite my disagreement with the principles of his assumptions. For those who prefer an Arabic version, I strongly recommend an excellent recent publication by Saint Macarius Monastery authored by Father Younan El-Makary titled *The Complete Works of Saint Macarius: The Fifty Homilies*.

I pray that you will enjoy the homilies of Macarius as much as I did, and learn more than I have, so that the one universal church will grow and our souls will be enlightened. May the intercessions of our lady, the Mother of God and the prayers of Saint Macarius be with us all, bringing fruit into the kingdom of God.

Chapter 1

St. Macarius of Egypt
300-391 AD

Macarius the Egyptian is highly esteemed in the Coptic Orthodox Church as a great saint as he is also known as Macarius the Great. He is deemed a saint and an influential spiritual father in the other Oriental Orthodox, the Eastern Orthodox, and Roman Catholic Churches. His teaching inspired many modern Christian preachers from outside the Orthodox tradition, such as John Wesley (1703-1791 AD) who established the Methodist Church in the UK.

The name Macarius (Makarios) in the Coptic language, as in Greek, means "blessed" and was a common name among Egyptians, especially in the fourth century. It is usually shortened to Makar or Makary. *The Egyptian* refers to someone who belonged to the indigenous race of Egypt; a Copt. This is to differentiate him from another saint who lived around the same time, Macarius the Alexandrian. *Alexandrian* refers to someone who belonged to the Greek colony in Alexandria. Though Macarius the Alexandrian was somewhat younger, both men became friends and stood out as giants of the ascetic life of that age and country. The third fourth century saint with the same name is Saint Marcius the Bishop who fought to maintain the Orthodox faith and was martyred in 451 AD. The three saints are mentioned collectively in the Coptic liturgy of Saint Basil, in the commemoration of the saints, as "the three holy Abba Makarii".

Early Life
Macarius the Egyptian was born in the village of Shobsheer (Shanshour- Ptinapor) in Lower Egypt, near the present city of Menouf around the year 300 AD. His father Abraham was a revered priest who served his community with enthusiasm and humility. His mother Sara was a wise and righteous woman who focused on supporting the poor people of their village. His parents received the good news about the birth of their blessed son in a vision when they saw an angel telling them that their son will be blessed and will have a multitude of righteous spiritual children. When Macarius was a young boy, he was ordained a deacon for his local church, a tradition which is still maintained by modern Coptic families all over the world. Initially, Macarius worked with his father in farming their land, but later he made his living by trading in saltpeter (Nitre, used as a fertilizer), which he brought from the area of Nitria. Here, he learnt many survival skills that became very handy when he later lived in the desolate desert.

When he became a young man, his parents frequently asked him to marry. Eventually, at the request of his parents, he married a young woman from his village, but the couple agreed to remain celibate. Shortly afterwards, his wife died, and he told himself; "Take heed, Macarius, and have care for your soul. It is fitting that you forsake the worldly life." One day the local bishop arrived at his village, having heard about his righteous manners, and ordained him a priest against his wishes. Later, he left his village and secretly went to another place to maintain his desire for a solitary life with Christ. He met an elder who taught him more about the way of righteousness and also the handicraft of weaving baskets, which later became the usual way for him and his future disciples to make their living. He lived in a hut on the outskirts of the village.

His Spiritual Test

The good Lord allowed a difficult temptation to test the saint's endurance and his determination to continue on his way. The son of the village chief fell in love with a young woman from his village who he wanted to marry, but his parents would not allow it because of the poor state of her family. When there was a feast in the village and people had plenty of fun and drink, the couple fell into the sin of sexual immorality. Later, when the girl's signs of pregnancy became evident, her lover advised her to say that it was Macarius who made her pregnant for he wished to protect himself and the reputation of his socially prominent family. When the villagers heard it, they attacked Macarius, beat him badly and paraded him in shame all around the whole village. The deacon who served him felt very ashamed of being associated with him. Macarius "looking unto Jesus, the author and finisher of our faith, who for the joy that was set before Him endured the cross, despising the shame" (Hebrews 12:2), did not attempt to defend himself, but kept silent as his Lord did (Mt 27:12). Eventually, they let him go after he agreed to pay all the expenses and maintenance for the girl and her future child. Having kept in his mind the advice of Sirach "Accept whatever brought on you, and in exchange for your humiliation, be patient; because gold is tested in fire and accepted men in the furnace of abasement" (Wisdom of Sirach 2:4-5), He told himself: "behold Makara, you now have a wife and a child. You have to work even harder to support them." He doubled his daily hand work so that he could afford her maintenance money. When the woman's delivery drew near, her labor became exceedingly difficult. She did not manage to give birth until she confessed Macarius' innocence. When the deacon heard it, he was very happy and ran to Macarius to inform him that the whole village was on their way to ask for his forgiveness as they have discovered his righteousness. When the multitude of people came out to his hut, they did not find him for he had fled in order to escape all worldly glory.

As he left he saw one of the Cherubim, full of eyes and with six wings, who reassured him of God's support and showed him the way to the Nitrian desert where he started his monastic life.

Meeting Saint Anthony the Great

Macarius lived in the Natrun valley in the Nitrian desert praying and serving God with all his heart. Three years later, as he realized that he needed more guidance and spiritual fatherhood, he decided to visit Anthony, who lived in the Eastern mountain by the Red Sea, to draw from his experience and benefit from his grace. Anthony was very happy to see him. Macarius told Anthony all his thoughts and intentions without keeping anything hidden. Anthony stood and kissed his head and said

"Macarius, you will be as blessed as the name given to you. You will be a great guide for many people and God will give you a multitude of spiritual children. My God has already revealed to me your ways and desires."

Anthony gave him the hand of fellowship and put on him the outfit of monks as he received it from an angel.

When Macarius returned to the Natrun valley, many people gathered around him and started his monastic community. They all lived separately in caves, cells and huts but they met every Sunday for the liturgy and Holy Communion while Macarius became their abbot, father and spiritual guide. They made their living by weaving baskets which they handed to a dealer, who would collect the baskets, sell them in the cities and villages and then buy the necessary needs for the monks, as the monks themselves would not normally go out of their monastic community to trade their handcraft. In a short period of time, his monastic community grew to be a few thousand monks who loved God and desired nothing but to please Him. Also, many people came regularly from Alexandria and from other cities to seek his blessing and guidance, especially as God gave him the gift of healing.

The two Roman princes

As his fame spread all over the Roman Empire, his virtue touched the hearts of the princes Maximus and Dometius who desired to live the monastic life and so left their kingdom to become his disciples. They were the sons of Valentinian, a Roman Emperor who feared God and was steadfast in his faith. When the Patriarch of Rome departed, they wanted to ordain Maximus in his place. His father rejoiced when he heard this. When the news reached Maximus and his brother, they disguised themselves and fled to Egypt to live under the guidance of Macarius who, when he first saw them, was reluctant to accept them because of their noble stature and the evidence of their life of luxury. He felt that they would not stand the harshness of the desert life. They answered him saying; "If we are not able to live here, we will return to where we came from." He then gave them a shovel and asked them to dig a cave for themselves in a nearby rock. Then he taught them how to plait palm leaves and told them about someone who would take their crafts to sell and then he left them.

They lived in the monastic community for three full years without seeking the company of anyone else. They only went to Church on Sundays to partake of the Holy Communion and left immediately afterwards. Macarius marveled that they did not go to him all these years to seek his advice. He visited them in their cave and delayed till they invited him to spend the night with them. He woke up at midnight to pray, as was his custom, and he saw the two saints praying and a ray of light like fire, going from their mouths to heaven. At dawn, they pretended they were asleep and they all got up to pray. Macarius dressed them with the holy outfit of the monks, and asked them to pray for him. Not many weeks later, Maximus became sick, and sent for Macarius to come and visit him again. When Macarius arrived, he found him ill with a fever. He blessed him before he passed away. After three days, Dometius also departed to heaven. Macarius went to their cave again and found him already dead, so he buried him next to his brother. Macarius used to take his monks to the cave of the two saints to remind them of their saintly way. He explained that the two princes did not need to come to him for any guidance as they were wise, perfect and humble; and they avoided all the other monks because that they did not want to make their righteousness known to anyone, so they would not be praised for attaining such a high spiritual level at their young age.

Two married women in Alexandria

After many years spent in ascetic living, while Macarius was praying, he heard a voice saying; "Macarius, you have not yet attained such perfection in virtue as two women who live in Alexandria." At once, he took his staff and went to the city and knocked at their house. The two women received him with joy and astonishment. As they questioned the reason for his unexpected visit, he said, "I have come from the desert seeking you in order to learn of your good deeds. Tell me your way to righteousness and do not hide anything." The two women answered with bewilderment,

> "we are not related but are married to two brothers. We love our husbands, and always look after our children without discriminating between them. After living together in one house for fifteen years, we have not uttered a single malicious nor disgraceful word, and we never quarrel among ourselves. We asked our husbands to allow us to enter a women's monastery, but they would not agree. We vowed not to utter a single worldly word until our death. We persevered together in our prayers and in our love for our husbands and children."

Macarius glorified God and said,
"in truth, the Lord seeks neither virgins nor married women, and neither monks nor married men, but He values a person's free will which He

accepts as the deed itself. He grants the grace of the Holy Spirit to everyone who believes, and the Holy Spirit works in accordance with each person's free will and directs the life of all who yearn to be saved."

His departure

Macarius lived until the age of ninety. Shortly before his death, Saint Anthony and Saint Pachomius appeared to him in a vision and told him that he will depart from this world in nine days. After instructing his disciples to persevere in the monastic rules and the traditions of the Fathers, he blessed them and began to prepare for his departure from this world. Macarius departed to the Lord saying, "into your hands, O Lord, I commit my spirit." He died in the year 391 AD. After his death, the natives of his village of Shabsheer took his body away and put it in a church they built in their village. Pope Michael V of Alexandria brought the relics of Saint Macarius back to the Nitrian Desert on 19th Mesra. Today, the body of Saint Macarius is found in his monastery, in Wadi El Natrun, Egypt, alongside the bodies of Saint Macarius the Alexandrian and Saint Macarius the Bishop.

The Coptic Church celebrates his departure to the heavens on 5th April (Baramhat 27), and the return of his body to his monastery (at the skete) on 25th August (Mesra 19). The Eastern Orthodox Church celebrates his feast day on 19th January (1st February according to the Julian Calendar). The Roman Catholic Church celebrates it on 15th January. May his blessings and payers be with us all so that we benefit from his teaching and imitate his life.

Chapter 2

Prepare Your Soul to be Christ's Throne

Homily 1: an allegorical interpretation of the vision written down by the Prophet Ezekiel.

The awesome vision of Ezekiel and its mysteries

1. In a spiritual experience higher than our minds can grasp, Ezekiel the prophet described his divine vision in human terms that were full of mystery. He saw a chariot of cherubim, that is four spiritual creatures. Each one had four faces:

> "each had the face of a man; each of the four had the face of a lion on the right side, each of the four had the face of an ox on the left side, and each of the four had the face of an eagle. Thus were their faces. Their wings stretched upward; two wings of each one touched one another, and two covered their bodies. And each one went straight forward; they went wherever the spirit wanted to go, and they did not turn when they went" (Ezk 1:10-12).

It seems as if they did not have front or back but they were completely full of eyes; there was no part of them that was not full of eyes. He also saw:

"a wheel was on the earth beside each living creature with its four faces. When they moved, they went toward any one of four directions; they did not turn aside when they went. As for their rims, they were so high they were awesome; and their rims were full of eyes, all around the four of them. When the living creatures went, the wheels went beside them; and when the living creatures were lifted up from the earth, the wheels were lifted up. Wherever the spirit wanted to go, they went, because there the spirit went; and the wheels were lifted together with them, for the spirit of the living creatures was in the wheels. When those went, these went; when those stood, these stood; and when those were lifted up from the earth, the wheels were lifted up together with them, for the spirit of the living creatures was in the wheels" (Ezk 1:15-21).

Ezekiel continued to illustrate in much detail:
"And above the firmament over their heads was the likeness of a throne, in appearance like a sapphire stone; on the likeness of the throne was a likeness with the appearance of a man high above it. Also from the appearance of His waist and upward I saw, as it were, the color of amber with the appearance of fire all around within it; and from the appearance of His waist and downward I saw, as it were, the appearance of fire with brightness all around. Like the appearance of a rainbow in a cloud on a rainy day, so was the appearance of the brightness all

around it. This was the appearance of the likeness of the glory of the Lord" (Ezk 1:26-28).

Ezekiel clearly saw the Lord in the likeness of a man riding a chariot and under His feet there was a beautifully artistic setting like sapphire. The cherubim and the living creatures pulled the chariot on which the Lord sat in whichever direction He wished to go. He merely pointed his face in that direction. Moreover, he saw the likeness of a hand of a man under the cherubim, carrying and supporting them.

The mysteries explained
2. Though all the prophet had seen was true and certain, it was a shadow of something else and a symbol of a hidden divine mystery; "the mystery which has been hidden from ages and from generations, but now has been revealed to His saints" (Col 1:26) in our time which is of the "last times" (1 Pet 1:20), that is since Christ appeared. Ezekiel revealed to us the mystery of the soul that would receive the Lord and become a throne for His glory. For the soul that is deemed worthy to be immersed in the light of the Lord and in the fellowship of the Holy Spirit, is covered with the beauty of the overwhelming glory of the Spirit; it becomes all light, all face, and all eye. There is no part of the soul that is not full of the spiritual eyes of light. That is to say, there is no part of the soul that is covered with darkness, as it has become totally light and spirit. The soul that has been enlightened is like the sun that is full of light from all around with no darkness in it. "For it is the God who commanded light to shine out of darkness, who has shone in our hearts to give the light of the knowledge of the glory of God in the face of Jesus Christ" (2 Cor 4:6). It becomes completely full of eyes, front and back, becoming all face,

and is lead forward by the glory of the Lord Himself, who mounts and rides upon the soul that has become His chariot of the cherubim. This is the privilege of being a dwelling place (Eph 2:22) and a throne of God, that the soul becomes all eye, all light, all face, all glory and all spirit, made so by Christ who drives, guides, carries, and supports the soul and adorns her with His spiritual beauty, for the Scripture says, "the hand of a man was underneath their wings on their four sides" (Ezk 1:8). This is why Christ is the one who carries the soul and still directs it on the way.

The four living creatures and the drives of the soul

3. The four living creatures that carry the chariot are a symbol for the four main driving forces that lead the soul: the free will, the conscience, the mind, and the emotions. As the eagle rules over all the other birds, the lion over all the wild beasts, the bull over the tamed animals and the man over all creatures, so those four driving forces rule over all the other faculties of the soul. In another way, such symbolism can also relate to the heavenly church of the saints. As the four living creatures were full of eyes (so many so that no one could number them), so the church of God that has been given to us all is given for the enjoyment of salvation, but no one can comprehend the depth of the church or the numbers of the saints in it but God alone. As the rider is carried by the chariot and the living creatures, in another way, He is carried by every soul that has become His throne and is full of eyes and light. This is similar to the vision portrayed in the book of the revelation of Saint John who said, "behold, He is coming with clouds" (Rev 1:7). The clouds here represent the saints who have become the thrones of God. This can also be seen in Saint Paul's letter to the Hebrews, which tells us that "we are surrounded

by so great a cloud of witnesses" (Heb 12:1).

The Lord rides the soul and guides it with the Spirit, directing it as He sees fit. Also, as the living creatures only go in the direction the rider wishes, so also our souls only go wherever the Lord guides them by His Spirit. He is the leader of our entire existence and takes us to wherever He wishes in our journey to heaven. At times, He works with the body and the thoughts. At other times, He leads the soul to the ends of the universe and shows it the revelations of hidden mysteries. What a good and wonderful leader He is, who will make us worthy of the glory of the resurrection, after He has glorified us, in our current life on earth, through our relationship with the Holy Spirit.

9. Therefore, let us ask Him to put to death our souls by His power that we may die to the world of darkness and live to Him. And let us ask Him also to take away from us the spirit of sin in order to receive the Holy Spirit that moves us from the wickedness of darkness into the light of Christ where we rest in eternal life. On the racecourse, the car that takes the lead becomes an obstacle in front of the other cars, preventing them from reaching the finishing line first, so similarly, the thoughts of righteousness and sin compete in a race in our minds. If the thought of sin gets the upper hand it becomes an obstacle, hindering the soul from approaching God who gives us victory over sin. But where God Himself truly rides and guides the soul, He always obtains the victory by directing and leading it in the right way. His expertise guides the chariot of the soul to obtain a heavenly mindset forever. In this way, God does not wage war directly against wickedness, but He guides us and gives us all power and authority so that we can be victorious in every way. As the cherubim do not go where they wish, but where the Rider directs them, so the holy souls are

led and guided by the Spirit of Christ who directs them wherever He wishes in their journey of victory. And, as wings give flight to the birds, so the heavenly light of the Spirit takes the thoughts of the soul to wherever He directs them.

Prayer: It is beyond my comprehension to understand how You make me Your throne. But You are the awesome God who created light out of darkness. Please change me to make me Your throne, guide me so that my whole existence inclines towards You, and support me in my journey to You with You. Give me the wings of Your Holy Spirit so that I fly to the place of Your heavenly rest and see my eternal inheritance. Without You, I can do nothing.

The Holy Spirit is our light who leads us to more light

4. Those souls that have been justified by the Lord have become heavenly light, as the Lord himself said; "You are the light of the world" (Mt 5:14). For He first transformed them into light, and then command them to be light to the world. He said:

> "Nor do they light a lamp and put it under a basket, but on a lampstand, and it gives light to all who are in the house. Let your light so shine before men, that they may see your good works and glorify your Father in heaven" (Mt 5:15-16).

That is to say; do not hide the gift that you have received from me, but give it to all who desire it. He also said:

> "The lamp of the body is the eye. If therefore your eye is good, your whole body will be full of light. But if your eye is bad, your whole body will be full of darkness. If therefore the light that is in

you is darkness, how great is that darkness!" (Mt 6:22-23).

Just as the eyes are the light of the body and when the eyes are healthy and sound, then the whole body is enlightened, so also the apostles, and all those who believed in the Lord Jesus through them, have been called to be the eyes and the light of the whole world. For this reason, the Lord says to all of us, "if you, who are the light of the world, will persevere in My faith and not turn away from My way, then the whole world will be enlightened by you. But if you, who are light, should be led into darkness, how great is that darkness, which is nothing more than the world." Thus, the apostles, who were made to be light, brought light to those who believed, and enlightened their hearts by the heavenly light of the Holy Spirit, the one who had enlightened them.

Prayer: My good Lord, You are the light of the world. Make me a heavenly light by Your Holy Spirit so that I can spread Your light to all those who are around me in every place I go. And make me a spiritual eye so they can see through me how wonderful you are rather than them seeing me condemn their darkness.

The Holy Spirit is our salt

5. In the same manner, Jesus said "you are the salt of the earth" (Mt 5:13), as He meant by "earth" the souls of all people. The apostles passed on to people the heavenly salt of the Holy Spirit, which seasons them to take away any decay and keep them free from every source of rot. Meat that is not salted will rot and produce a stench, moreover worms will crawl and burrow in it, so that people will turn away from it and throw it away. But if it is salted it will not rot as the salt

will cure it and prevent decay. In the same manner, every soul that is not seasoned with the salt of the Holy Spirit grows corrupt and is filled with the stench of bad thoughts, so that God turns His face away from the awful stench of vain thoughts and dark emotions that dwell in such a soul. That soul will be attacked by worms, which are the spirits of wickedness and the powers of darkness, crawling up and down devouring such a soul as it is written, "my wounds are foul and festering because of my foolishness" (Ps 38:5). But, if the soul returns to God, the Spirit who loves people and who is the salt of life, then this heavenly salt comes and destroys those ugly worms, taking away the awful stench and cleansing the soul by the strength of His power. Thus, the soul is brought back to a healthy state of well-being and freed from its damaging lusts by the true salt and then it becomes fit to serve the Heavenly Lord again. That is why God, in the Law of Moses, ordered that all sacrifices be salted with salt (Lev 2:13). And Jesus explained to us that "everyone will be seasoned with fire, and every sacrifice will be seasoned with salt" (Mk 9:49). He warned us about losing our seasoning that we have received form the Holy Spirit, saying "salt is good, but if the salt loses its flavor, how will you season it? Have salt in yourselves" (Mk 9:50).

Prayer: Jesus, you are the salt of the earth, season me with Your salt that will take away all my rotten thoughts, infectious sins and all the worms of hidden lusts. I do not ever want to be salt that has lost its flavor and is good for nothing. Give me a new life that is seasoned by Your Heavenly Spirit.

6. In the Law of Moses, God commanded that the priest should first kill every sacrifice, then season it with salt before placing it on the fire. This is to say that unless the priest first kills the lamb, it will not be salted nor will

it be brought to the Lord as a burnt offering. In the same manner, our souls must come to Christ, our High Priest, to be slain by Him and die to the world and to sin, for the life of wicked passions must be expelled out of the soul. Our Lord Jesus is not like any other high priest, but as Saint Paul said:

> "we have a great High Priest who has passed through the heavens, Jesus the Son of God, let us hold fast our confession. For we do not have a High Priest who cannot sympathize with our weaknesses, but was in all points tempted as we are, yet without sin" (Heb 4:14-15).

When Christ, our Heavenly High Priest, puts to death our worldly life, it dies to the life of corruption that it formerly lived. It no longer hears, nor speaks, nor moves about in the darkness of sin because it has been made dead to the world. Thus, the apostle exclaims, saying; "the world has been crucified to me and I to the world" (Gal 6:14). For the soul which still lives in the world and in the darkness of sin, has not yet been put to death, but still harbors the source of the dark passions of sin. But those who are nurtured by the Body of Christ, possess the source of light that is the Holy Spirit, who gives them the power to say with Saint Paul:

> "I have been crucified with Christ; it is no longer I who live, but Christ lives in me; and the life which I now live in the flesh I live by faith in the Son of God, who loved me and gave Himself for me" (Gal 2:20).

The light of the Holy Spirit rather than the garment of darkness

7. When Adam violated the command of God and obeyed the deceitful serpent, he sold himself to the devil that put a garment of darkness over his soul. Therefore, the soul that is held captive by sin is considered to be a body of darkness and wickedness, as Saint Paul called it the body of sin (Rom 6:6). This was the very reason why the Lord came, to give man a new nature that "is renewed in knowledge according to the image of Him who created him" (Col 3:10) and to reclaim His temple that is our body. "Your body is the temple of the Holy Spirit who is in you" (1 Cor 6:19). On the other hand, the soul that truly believes in God and has been freed from the darkness of sin and accepts the light of the Holy Spirit as its source of life, has passed from death to life. Thereafter, the soul that is saved spends its life in the Spirit for it is now strongly held captive by divine light. That is what Jesus achieved on the cross when He

> "wiped out the handwriting of requirements that was against us, which was contrary to us. And He has taken it out of the way, having nailed it to the cross. Having disarmed principalities and powers, He made a public spectacle of them, triumphing over them in it" (Col 2:14-15).

The soul is neither divine by nature, nor is it part of the darkness of wickedness by nature, but it was created intellectual, beautiful, unique and admirable, as it was created in the image of God. Only through violating God's commandments the soul is turned into the image of wickedness and the passions of darkness.

8. Saint Paul explains to us that "he who is joined to a harlot is one body with her," quoting our Lord who reminds us that the two shall become one flesh (1 Cor

6:16), while "he who is joined to the Lord is one spirit with Him" (1 Cor 6:17). Therefore, the soul is one with whatever it is joined to. Either it is united with God and therefore has the light of God in it and lives in that divine light with all of His powers, or it is united with Satan, and therefore is permeated by the darkness of sin. When we die to the world, our life's desires and pleasures change completely. Like when someone dies in a city, he or she is unable to hear the voices of others around him or her, but is completely dead and buried in a place where there are no voices or noises of the city. In the same way, the soul, after it has been slain by the true High Priest becomes dead to that city of evil passions where it once earlier lived, and no longer hears inside itself the voice of troubling thoughts nor desires any of its previous hidden or manifest pleasures. It no longer gets involved in silly arguments. For it has moved to the city that is full of goodness and peace, to the city of divine light. There it lives, listens, speaks, and communicates with the Lord and performs all the spiritual works that are truly worthy of God.

10,11. God created our body to get its supplies such as food, drink, clothing and footwear from sources outside it. We were created naked and powerless. Therefore, we could not live without things that come from sources external to our nature. In the same manner, our souls need to take eternal life from the Holy Spirit. This does not come from our own nature, as the Lord said

> "unless you eat the flesh of the Son of Man and drink His blood, you have no life in you. Whoever eats My flesh and drinks My blood has eternal life, and I will raise him up at the last day" (Jn 6:53-54).

As the body does not have life in itself, but

receives the supplies of life from outside, that is, from the earth—and without such material things it cannot live—so also the soul cannot live safely unless it is reborn into the "land of the living" (Ps 27:13) where it is fed spiritually and grows in the grace of the Lord and is clothed in the beauty of the heavenly garments that flow out of the Holy Trinity. It is not because of the soul's own nature but because of God's divinity, of His very Spirit and of His light, that our souls receive their spiritual food, drink and heavenly clothing which are truly the life of the soul. For the source of life is in the divine nature who describes Himself as the bread of life (Jn 6:35), the living water (Jn 4:10), the wine which "gladdens the heart of man, to brighten his face with oil" (Ps 104:15) and the light of the world (Jn 8:12). All this food of the heavenly Spirit comes from God. Indeed, this is the source of the eternal life of the soul.

Woe to the body if it relies solely on its own nature, because then, by nature, it withers and dies. Woe also to the soul that tries to find all its existence in its own nature and that trusts solely in its own abilities, refusing the fellowship of the Divine Spirit because in this way it will not experience the eternal and divine life. For just as it happens to sick men that when their bodies no longer desire food, all their friends and relatives grieve and lose hope for their survival, so also God and all the holy angels are saddened to see those who do not eat the heavenly food of the Spirit and do not seek the real source of life. These things are not simply spoken words, but they are the work of the spiritual life, the work of truth, which works in worthy and faithful souls.

Prayer: My Lord, You know that there is no life in me as I am "wretched, miserable, poor, blind, and naked" (Rev 3:17). You are my true and only hope. Please, take the darkness out of me, make me all light and all eyes; season me with Your Spirit, nourish me with Your body, water me with Your precious blood, clothe me with the glory of Your Holy Spirit so that my soul becomes a living throne for You, and I taste Your heavenly life and prepare for my eternity with You.

Our eternal life on earth

12. If you have become a throne of God and the Lord is the only master over you, if your whole soul has become a spiritual eye and has become totally light, and if you have been nourished with the heavenly food of the Spirit and you have drunk from the water of life, and if you have put on the garment of indescribable light and are rooted in the abundance of faith, then you already live in eternal life and your soul rests in the Lord. You have truly received all these things from the Lord so that you may live life truly in Him. But if you have not experienced any of these things, weep and mourn because you have not yet been made a partaker of eternal riches and you have not yet received true life.

If you have been made aware by the Spirit of God of your own poverty and shortfalls, do not be complacent but ask the Lord day and night to give you this true divine life, and you will soon obtain redemption and heavenly riches, just as the Lord said in His story of the unjust judge and the widow; "shall not God avenge His own elect who cry out day and night to Him, though He bears long with them? I tell you that He will avenge them speedily" (Lk 18:7-8).

To Him be glory and power forever. Amen.

Chapter 3

New Clothes for the New Man

Homily 2: On the reign of darkness, that is, of sin and that God is capable of taking sin away from us and freeing us from the slavery to the evil prince.

The clothes of darkness and the clothes of light

1. After humanity at the beginning was taken captive by the kingdom of darkness, Satan surrounded the soul and clothed it with darkness. As in the olden days, when they made someone a king, they clothed him with royal garments from head to foot, so likewise Satan clothed the soul with the darkness of sin, till he corrupted it completely, not sparing any of its thoughts or parts from its bondage. Neither did he spare the mind nor the body, but he clothed it all with darkness. As when one part of the body suffers, the whole body suffers, so the entire soul was subjected to the desires of evil and sin. Satan thus clothed the whole soul with his own wickedness, that is, with sin. And so, the entire body fell victim to passion and corruption.

2. When Saint Paul tells us to "put off the old man" (Eph 4:22), he refers indeed to the entire man; having new eyes in place of the old eyes, new ears replacing the old ears, new hands for old hands and new intentions for old intentions. For the wicked one has defiled the entire person, soul and body, and dragged him or her down, making him or her polluted, impure, and an enemy of God, "not subject to the law of God" (Rom 8:7). The old man is ruled by sin, so that he can no longer see freely but his sight, hearing and desires are corrupted by evil, he has swift feet and hands to do evil acts and his heart ponders evil deeds. Isaiah the prophet describes the state of the old man saying; "their feet run to evil, and they make haste to shed innocent blood; their thoughts are thoughts of iniquity; wasting and destruction are in their paths" (Is 59:7).

Let us therefore beg God to take off from us the old man, because He alone is able to take sin away from us. Those who captured us and forced us into this sad state are stronger than us, but God, who has promised us that He would free us from this slavery, is capable of fulfilling His promise as He said; "if the Son makes you free, you shall be free indeed" (Jn 8:36). We all should be like Abraham who believed that; "what He had promised He was also able to perform" (Rom 4:21). For the sun shines and the wind blows together, each having its own state and nature, yet no one can separate the wind from the sun (but God alone can calm the wind so it blows no more). Similarly, sin is also mixed with the soul even though each has its own nature. It is, therefore, impossible to separate the soul from sin unless God calms and turns back this evil wind that inhabits both the soul and the body.

Wings to fly very high

3. Anyone who watches a bird flying may wish that he himself could fly, yet still he cannot fly, as he does not have wings. So also, a man may have the desire to be pure, without blame and spotless, to be always in communion with God, yet he does not truly have this power. Someone may desire to fly into divine places to enjoy the liberty of the Holy Spirit (2 Cor 3:18), but if he or she is not given wings, this is not possible. Let us pray to God that He may give us the "wings like a dove" (Ps 55:6), of the Holy Spirit so we may fly to Him and find rest. All the more we should pray that He may take away from our soul and body the sin that dwells in us. For He alone is able to do so, as it says: "behold, the Lamb of God who takes away the sins of the world" (Jn 1:29). Jesus alone has shown this mercy to those who believe in him by redeeming them from sin, for He always presents his profound salvation to those who continuously wait for Him and diligently seek Him, putting all their hope on Him. "Now may the God of hope fill you with all joy and peace in believing, that you may abound in hope by the power of the Holy Spirit" (Rom 15:13).

Prayer: My Lord, take off the old man and give me new eyes, new ears, new hands and feet and a new mind that is renewed according to Your will. Make me a completely new man in You. And, while you are working on me, please give me two wings for my soul to fly to You and taste eternal life with You. Give me Your Holy Spirit to cleanse me and unite me with You as You promised. I ask You to make everything new that I may say with all Your saints; "old things have passed away; behold, all things have become new" (2 Cor 5:17). I believe that You will fulfil Your promise in me.

Eyes instead of eyes and ears instead of ears
4. As in a dark gloomy night when a strong wind blows and strikes all the plants shaking them vigorously, so also man, who has fallen under the power of the night of the devil of darkness, is battered and shaken by the stiff wind of sin influencing his soul, heart and mind. All the members of the body are shaken; not one part of the soul or the body is immune from the passions of sin dwelling in us as Isaiah described:

> "The whole head is sick, and the whole heart faints. From the sole of the foot even to the head, there is no soundness in it, but wounds and bruises and putrefying sores; They have not been closed or bound up, or soothed with ointment" (Is 1:5-6).

In a similar way, there is a day of light when the divine breeze of the Holy Spirit breathes refreshment on the souls who live according to God's love and commandments. The divine breeze passes through the whole nature of the person; through the thoughts and the entire substance of the soul and all the members of the body, recreating and refreshing them with overwhelming divine tranquility. This is what the apostle said "we are not sons of the night nor of the darkness, for you all are sons of light and sons of the day" (1 Thess 5:5). Just as in the state of sin and error, the old man puts on the complete garment of the kingdom of darkness, the cloak of blasphemy, unbelief, pride, greed, sexual immorality, lust, and all the other similar snares of the kingdom of darkness, so here, on the contrary, all who have put off the old man (who Jesus has removed the clothing of the kingdom of darkness from) have put on the new and heavenly man, Jesus Christ Himself. So that, once again, the old eyes are changed to new eyes, old ears to new ears, old hands to new hands and old mind to new mind in order to be completely pure, bearing the heavenly image. This is what Saint Paul explains to us "as we have borne the image of the man of dust, we shall also bear the image of the heavenly Man" (1 Cor 15:49).

Prayer: My Lord, fill me with your Holy Spirit who will take away all the darkness and sin from my deep parts and enlighten me with Your divine light that will guide me in my journey to Your kingdom. As You have already invited me to your heavenly wedding, please take away the cloak of darkness that the devil has put on me when I previously obeyed him. Instead, provide me with the wedding garments as I cannot attend the wonderful eternal wedding with You without them.

5. These who have put off the old man are those the Lord has clothed with the garments of the kingdom of indescribable light; the garments of faith, hope, love, joy, peace, goodness, human warmth, and all the other divine garments of light. The result is that, as God is love, joy, peace, kindness and goodness, so too the new man will be by grace. These are the garments that we need to wear to enter the wedding of the son of God, but those who try to enter without them will hear His voice saying; "Friend, how did you come in here without a wedding garment?" and as they don't have an answer to this, they will hear Him instructing his angels "bind him hand and foot, take him away, and cast him into outer darkness; there will be weeping and gnashing of teeth" (Mt 22:11-13). And just as the kingdom of darkness and sin are hidden in the soul until the day of resurrection when the very bodies of sinners will be covered over with the darkness that is already inside them, so also the kingdom of light and the heavenly image, Jesus Christ, now mystically illuminates the souls of all His children. Indeed, Christ is hidden from the eyes of men, until the

day of resurrection, when the body itself will reign with the soul, which then, having attained the Kingdom of Christ, will be filled with the light of the Holy Spirit.

Glory to His compassion and mercy for He shows pity on His servants, enlightens and frees them from the kingdom of darkness. He bestows on them light and His kingdom. To Him be glory and power forever and ever. Amen.

Chapter 4

Into the Image of Him Who Died for Us

Homily 4: Christians ought to run their race in this world with much diligence and care, that they may gain divine commendation from God and His angels.

We need discernment to complete the journey safely
1-5 Those who strive to live a true Christian life must, above all, develop their soul's ability to understand and discern what is right. When we have acquired the ability to differentiate between good and evil, we may conduct ourselves properly and without offense. This ability to distinguish what is right becomes like an eye, so that we can escape all fellowship with evil and receive the divine gift of the Holy Spirit and so become worthy to be with the Lord.

There is indeed a similarity between the body and the soul, and between the things of the body and the things of the soul. For instance, the body has the eye as a guide, which, by seeing, keeps the whole body on the right path. It is like someone who travels through the woods, who risks injuring himself or at least getting his clothes dirty unless his eye guides him carefully. But if anyone goes through the woods being lazy or careless, in one way or another, he quickly ruins his elegant clothes. Moreover, if he is not diligent and alert to where his eye leads him, he might fall into a ditch or even drown in a creek. In the same way also the soul, which is clothed with an attractive garment—namely the body—possesses the ability to distinguish between good and evil, and this acts as an eye to direct the soul, together with the body, as it passes through the scum and the thorns of this life, that is, the lusts and pleasures of this world. The soul should also wrap around itself vigilance, diligence, courage, attentiveness, and self-control, so that it will not be torn by thorns in the woods of this world, which represent anxieties, fears, bodily lusts, worldly cares and earthly worries.

The soul indeed has the will to turn away from participating in inappropriate deeds to keep away from hearing what is an evil and improper, and distance itself from every indecent conversation and worldly chat. Therefore, the soul that disciplines itself and turns away from all mental distractions, keeping the heart from pondering worldly thoughts, is freed by the Lord from all ripping sin. And so, the soul preserves itself, through its willful choices, and remains completely pure for the Lord who provides help and protection from every evil. For whenever the Lord sees anyone courageously turning away from sinful pleasures, distractions and worldly ties, and from preoccupation with vain ambitions, He gives that person His special help through the grace of the Holy Spirit and protects the soul throughout its journey in this present corrupt world. But if anyone journeys through this life in a lazy manner, negligent in turning away from all worldly lust and seeking his or her own will (instead of seeking only the Lord), his or her garment (that is the body) will be soiled with the muck of sensuous pleasures. And the soul without such confidence is found lacking "boldness in the day of judgment" (1 Jn 4:17), because it did not preserve its clothing unsoiled, but rather soiled it with the deceits of this world. And for this reason, it is cast out from the kingdom. God indeed helps those who turns away from sleazy pleasures and from their former unhelpful habits; who always focus all their thoughts on the Lord; who deny themselves and continuously seek the Lord eagerly. These are those who God takes care of and guards from the snares and enticements of the woods of this world as they work out their "own salvation with fear and trembling" (Phil 2:12).

We also need the oil of the Holy Spirit

6-8. Jesus revealed to us essential secrets to help us on our way to heaven when He told us about the five wise virgins saying;

> "the kingdom of heaven shall be likened to ten virgins who took their lamps and went out to meet the bridegroom. Now five of them were wise, and five were foolish. Those who were foolish took their lamps and took no oil with them, but the wise took oil in their vessels with their lamps. But while the bridegroom was delayed, they all slumbered and slept. And at midnight a cry was heard: 'Behold, the bridegroom is coming; go out to meet him!' Then all those virgins arose and trimmed their lamps. And the foolish said to the wise, 'Give us some of your oil, for our lamps are going out.' But the wise answered, saying, 'No, lest there

should not be enough for us and you; but go rather to those who sell, and buy for yourselves.' And while they went to buy, the bridegroom came, and those who were ready went in with him to the wedding; and the door was shut. Afterward the other virgins came also, saying, 'Lord, Lord, open to us!' But he answered and said, 'Assuredly, I say to you, I do not know you.' Watch therefore, for you know neither the day nor the hour in which the Son of Man is coming" (Mt 25:1-13).

It is obvious that those five prudent, vigilant virgins received in their hearts something that was not from their own nature. This is the oil of the Holy Spirit, which enabled them to enter the kingdom of Heaven together with the Bridegroom. But people who have failed to acquire the Holy Spirit through their laziness, negligence or ignorance are like the five foolish virgins who were excluded from the wedding of the lamb, as they were content with their own fallen nature and were bound by attachments to the world and by earthly love. They did not offer their love and devotion fully to the heavenly spouse nor did they carry with them "the oil of gladness" (Ps 45:7 and Heb 1:9).

We also need proper wedding clothes
The souls who seek the sanctification of the Holy Spirit, which lies beyond their natural power, are completely bound to the Lord with a wholehearted love. There they walk with Him; there they pray; there they focus their thoughts, ignoring all the fuzziness of the world. Those who have not been born of the Spirit from above (Jn 3:3) and are not true Christians, but only take on the external appearance of the true Christians through empty words, false humility and meaningless

rituals are like those Jesus found unworthy to attend His heavenly wedding. For "'blessed are those who are called to the marriage supper of the Lamb!' And he said to me, 'These are the true sayings of God.'" (Rev 19:9). But He also taught us that in the King's wedding all were invited but

> "when the king came in to see the guests, he saw a man there who did not have on a wedding garment. So, he said to him, 'Friend, how did you come in here without a wedding garment?' And he was speechless. Then the king said to the servants, 'Bind him hand and foot, take him away, and cast him into outer darkness; there will be weeping and gnashing of teeth'" (Mt 22:11-13).

When our five rational senses receive grace from above to be sanctified by the Holy Spirit, they become like the genuine wise virgins. But if they continue to depend solely on their own nature, they classify themselves with the foolish virgins.

And we need something that we never had before

When we fell into sin, we received inside ourselves something that was foreign to our nature, namely, the corruption of our desires through the disobedience of the first man. This corrupted nature can only be expelled by something that is also foreign to our nature, that is the Holy Spirit. In this way, our original purity must be restored in the image of God as He created us in the first place. Unless we truly receive the Holy Spirit, we will not be able to obtain the heavenly kingdom and will be kept out like the five foolish virgins and the guest who tried to attend the wedding without the proper wedding garment. Therefore, let us ask Him to fill us with His Holy Spirit as He said:

"ask, and it will be given to you; seek, and you will find; knock, and it will be opened to you. For everyone who asks receives, and he who seeks finds, and to him who knocks it will be opened. If a son asks for bread from any father among you, will he give him a stone? Or if he asks for a fish, will he give him a serpent instead of a fish? Or if he asks for an egg, will he offer him a scorpion? If you then, being evil, know how to give good gifts to your children, how much more will your heavenly Father give the Holy Spirit to those who ask Him!" (Lk 11:10 - 13).

Prayer: My dear Lord, I need something which does not come from my nature which is capable of transforming me into Your image; I need Your Holy Spirit to give me life, to dress me with wedding clothes and to fill me with the oil of gladness which will keep me watching out for Your arrival. I know You listen to all of us who genuinely ask this from You and knock on Your door. Please fill all of us, Your children, with Your Holy Spirit as You promised.

God truly and deeply loves all of us
9-13. The almighty God, who far exceeds the grasp of our human understanding, diminished Himself through His goodness and took our human body so that His visible creatures could be united with Him. In His great love, He accepts the lowliness of being one Spirit with those who are united with Him, as Saint Paul said, "he who is joined to the Lord is one spirit with Him" (1 Cor 6:17). This is how our souls can obtain new, immortal life and participate in His eternal glory. God created all visible creatures out of nothing. He created all things with great variations in different forms and shapes. He willed and with no effort created solid, hard

things out of nothing, for example the earth, the mountains and the trees, which are obviously very hard things. He created water and even more subtle things, such as fire and wind. It is an amazing mystery that God, who created all things out of nothing, diminished Himself and took on a body. By this body, He, the invisible, can be seen by our souls. He, who is untouchable, may thus be touched by us. In this way, also our souls may taste His sweetness and enjoy the goodness of His light. This experience gives inexpressible pleasure. When God wishes, He becomes fire, burning up every abrasive desire that has taken root in the soul "for our God is a consuming fire" (Deut 4:24, Heb 12:29). When He wishes, He becomes a mysterious rest so that the soul may find rest in God's rest. When He wishes, He becomes joy and peace, protecting the soul. All things are easy and possible for Him who can transform Himself into any form that He wishes for the benefit of those souls who are worthy and faithful to Him. God appeared to each of the holy fathers as it seemed helpful to them. He appeared to Abraham in one way, and in other ways to Isaac, Jacob, Noah, Daniel, David, Solomon, Isaiah and Elijah. He appeared in yet another way to Moses who was fasting for forty days on the mountaintop and approached the spiritual table and feasted on many delights. To each of the saints, God appeared as He wished so as to refresh them, and to save and lead them into His knowledge. For all things are easy for Him. When it pleased Him, He emptied himself by taking on a bodily form. He transforms himself to become visible to the eyes of those who truly love him. In His utmost love for us, the Lord transforms Himself into bread and drink as it is written in the Gospel, "he who eats this bread will live forever" (Jn 6:58). In this indescribable mystery, He recreates the soul and fills it with spiritual happiness. For

He says; "I am the bread of life" (Jn 6:35). Similarly, He transforms himself into drink from a heavenly fountain as He says:

> "Whoever drinks of the water that I shall give him will never thirst. But the water that I shall give him will become in him a fountain of water springing up into everlasting life" (Jn 4:14).

And it is also said that we all drink of "the same spiritual drink" (1 Cor 10:4, 12:13).

Prayer: My God, as if it was not enough that You have taken a human body to allow me to see You and touch You, You invite me to be united with You in a mysterious way to transform me to conform to Your way. Moreover, You gave me Your holy body and Your precious blood to feed me from the divine source of life. It is certainly above me, how You make Yourself apparent to me only in the way that suits my need and ability to comprehend Your call for me.

The love of the Holy Spirit changes our nature

14-16 Iron, gold or silver melts when thrown into the fire and is transformed from its hard nature to a soft substance as long as it remains in the fire. The same is true for the soul that receives that heavenly fire of the Holy Spirit; it is then truly freed from all attachments to the world and liberated from every evil affection. For "the Lord is the Spirit; and where the Spirit of the Lord is, there is liberty" (2 Cor 3:17). As the soul rejects the lusts and desires of this world, all its natural harsh characteristics change by the love of the heavenly bridegroom to the sweetness and gentleness of Him who died for it.

Those who found their partners and married them, have left behind all other loves including their natural love for their parents in order to be one with the person they love. For such an earthly love can easily and rightly separate the married couple from their parents, family and friends as all other things become rather secondary for them because of their deep love for each other, for it is said: "therefore a man shall leave his father and mother and be joined to his wife, and they shall become one flesh" (Gen 2:24). If earthly love can detach people from all their other loves, how much more can the love of the Holy Spirit? Those who are filled with the love of the Holy Spirit are freed from all worldly love. All other things seem indifferent to them since they have been captured by a heavenly love, becoming one with the God who they surrendered to.

The Lord, who is the lover of mankind, is full of tender compassion, and is always waiting for us to turn to Him completely in order to be freed from all darkness and evil. Even though we, in our supreme ignorance, childishness and tendency towards evil, move away from Him, placing many obstructions along our path because of our reluctance to repent, nevertheless, He continues to have great mercy on us. He patiently waits for us until we are converted by Him and sanctified in Him that our faces may not be ashamed in the day of judgment as it is said, "for both He who sanctifies and those who are being sanctified are all of one, for which reason He is not ashamed to call them brethren" (Heb 2:11).

Therefore, dearest brothers and sisters, since such good things have been offered to us and such wonderful promises have been made to us by the Lord, let us get rid of every hurdle that stands between Him and us. Like King Josiah "who turned to the Lord with all his heart, with all his soul, and with all his might" (2 Kings 23:24-26), let us renounce any love for the world, for friendship with the world is enmity with God; "whoever therefore wants to be a friend of the world makes himself an enemy of God" (Jm 4:4). Let us devote ourselves to carefully seek and long for the one who saved us, so that we may share in the indescribable love of the Spirit which Saint Paul told us about when he urged us to "pursue love and desire spiritual gifts" (1 Cor 14:1). Having been touched by the love of the divine Spirit, we may be converted by the right hand of the Most High from our hard nature to a new spiritual sweetness. This is how we can find rest in Him as He promised: "I will give you a new heart and put a new spirit within you; I shall take the heart of stone out of your flesh and give you a heart of flesh" (Ezk 36:26).

His goodness and forbearance lead us to repentance

17-23. Satan, our adversary "walks about like a roaring lion, seeking whom he may devour" (1 Pet 5:8). This suggests to us that the road of practicing righteousness is hard. But our good shepherd, who always works for our salvation, is full of compassion, tolerance and patience as He waits for us to change. When we do sin, He is ready to lift us up as He desires our repentance. When we fall, He is not ashamed to take us back, as the prophet said; "Will they fall and not rise? Will one turn away and not return?" (Jr 8:4). How is it possible that in the face of so many encouragements and promises, we still refuse to surrender ourselves completely to Him? Our Lord Jesus said; "You shall love the Lord your God with all your heart, with all your soul, and with all your mind" (Mt 22:37). What a great mercy that the Lord has been shown to us from the very beginning! Finally, by coming to our earth He has shown to us His deep kindness through His crucifixion in order to convert us into His image. We certainly need "to be conformed to the image of His Son, that He might be the firstborn among many brethren" (Rom 8:29). And yet, we do not have the will to give up our love for the world nor our evil tendencies and habits because we have only a little faith. In spite of all this, He still loves, protects and cherishes us, not turning us over (according to the wages of our sin) to the deceits of evil which are in the world He watches over us from above in His great compassion and patience, waiting for the time we shall return to Him. My dear brothers and sisters, I fear that the saying of the apostle might be fulfilled in us; "do you despise the riches of His goodness, forbearance, and longsuffering, not knowing that the goodness of God leads you to repentance?" (Rom 2:4). But if we abuse the patience, kindness and tolerance of God, we add still more sins to those we already have, and store up for ourselves more serious judgments, that the saying will be fulfilled:

> "in accordance with your hardness and your impenitent heart you are treasuring up for yourself wrath in the day of wrath and revelation of the righteous judgment of God" (Rom 2:5).

Consider the Israelite fathers to whom the promises were made, from whom Christ in the flesh came, to whom "the adoption, the glory, the covenants" (Rom 9:4) belonged. How much have they sinned? How many times did they turn away from God? Nevertheless, He did not abandon them, but sent them the prophets. Only when they committed the great sin of laying hands on their very own Lord whom they were expecting and inflicted on Him the punishment of the cross, they reached the fullness of their crime. And thus, finally they were deserted as He told them, "See! Your house is left to you desolate" (Mt 23:38). The Holy Spirit left them when the veil of the temple was torn in two. And so, their Temple was handed over to the Gentiles, destroyed and made desolate according to the Lord's saying, "not one stone shall be left here upon another, that shall not be thrown down" (Mt 24:2). They lost the prophecy and the priesthood of God. These were given to the believing Gentiles as the Lord says "the Kingdom of God shall be taken from you and given to a nation bearing the fruits of it" (Mt 21:43).

God, who is good and kind, and patient with each one of us, sees how much each of us offends Him and yet He quietly waits until each is converted from sin, and then He is filled with great love and joy. This explains the verses which say "there will be more joy in heaven over one sinner who repents than over ninety-nine just persons who need no repentance" (Lk 15:7) and, "it is not the will of your Father who is in heaven that one of these little ones should perish" (Mat 18:14). So, if anyone receives such immense goodness and gentleness from God, who is reaching out to him or her, and still does not accept the pardoning of his or her every offense, hidden or visible, then this person abuses God's kindness by remaining hardened in his or her sins. This person is like the people who committed great sins and refused to repent in the days of Noah. They fell into such enormous sins that finally the whole earth perished. Sometime after, the Egyptians offended God greatly by committing sins against God's people. God still showed them His mercy by not totally destroying them. Instead, He inflicted on them smaller plagues as a warning, for their correction to lead them to repentance. He bore with them patiently, waiting for their conversion. But they sinned in many ways against God after that. Even when they showed some willingness to repent, they later changed their minds. Finally, when God led his people out of Egypt with great miracles, together with Moses their leader, they committed the serious sin of pursuing God's people. God's judgement completely destroyed them in the Red Sea.

If we simply have a sincere heart, live in vigilance and are ready to be changed to become partakers of the divine nature, He himself is always ready and willing to immediately save us when we seek His help. For He looks for our eager desire to turn to Him as best we can. When we desire to turn to Him in true faith and genuine readiness, then He truly converts us "for it is God who works in you both to will and to do for His good pleasure" (Phil 2:13). Let us then, dear friends, show diligence as children of God, and be swift to follow Him. Let us cast aside all worldly preoccupation, laziness and carelessness, not postponing day after day this work which prevents evil from controlling us. For we do not know the hour at which we will have to leave this life. Great and indescribable are the promises offered to true Christians. They are so great, indeed, that all the glory and beauty of heaven and earth cannot measure up to the beauty and riches of a single Christian soul. Therefore, it is said, "work out your own salvation with fear and trembling" (Phil 2:12).

Prayer: My Lord, Your mercy and love are beyond my comprehension. You have not only waited for me to repent while I was offending You but You also planned to change me into Your image when I returned to You. Give me Your love, to cover me like a banner, and the courage to stand firm against the evil one who wants to remind me of my sins. Please give me diligence in my journey so that I reject all worldly desires and give me a heart that fully trusts You and Your love and care for me.

We must reject despair, hopelessness and helplessness and return swiftly to our God who is always waiting for us with His arms open

24-27 The remembrance of our past sins can easily lead us to despair, laziness, negligence, and the assumption that we may never be converted back to the Lord and so never attain salvation, even though the great goodness of the Lord covers the multitude of sins of the whole human race. Therefore, let us now consider this seriously, remembering how our Lord, while on this earth, restored sight to the blind, cured the paralyzed man, cleansed the woman who had a flow of blood, healed every sickness and raised a dead man who was already decaying and disintegrating. So, how much more will He accept and convert a soul that turns back to Him, seeking his mercy and help? Will He not give freedom from wrong desires to such a soul and renew its mind? Will He not lead this soul to the true light and fill it with insight, freeing it from blindness, deafness, uncleanness, sickness and the death of unbelief? For God, who created the body, also made the soul. When He walked on this earth, He gave help and health to those who approached Him, asking for such favors. He granted healing to everyone with generosity and kindness for He is the good physician and the only one who is true. So, we can see how He will act in the same way when it comes to spiritual matters and our eternal life!! If God was so moved with such great mercy towards human bodies which were going to die and dissolve, how much more mercy will He show to an immortal soul that is overwhelmed by the sickness of ignorance, the wickedness of lust, unfaithfulness and arrogance, and all the other passions of sin? Will He not give His healing freedom more quickly and promptly according to his word, as He said, "shall God not avenge His own elect who cry out day and night to Him, though He bears long with them? I tell you that He will avenge them speedily" (Lk 18:7-8).

This is all to say that God nudges us to seek His gift of grace continually and without shame. He indeed came for sinners, to convert them and turn them back to Himself and to bring healing to all who would believe in Him. As He said, "I did not come to call the righteous, but sinners, to repentance" (Mt 9:13). Let us have nothing to do with wicked and vain talk, but let us cling to Him in all things with all our might. For He is certainly always ready to give us all His help. He heals incurable desires and gives redemption to those who call on Him, who turn away from all worldly desires as best as they can, freely choosing to force their minds away from earthly cares and to eagerly hold fast to Him. And thus, they obtain the heavenly gift of the Holy Spirit through this faith, and the Holy Spirit helps them to make daily progress in goodness and in perseverance to the end, which is the way of righteousness. Therefore, those people never offend Him again in any matter. They are deemed worthy to receive eternal salvation with all the saints who they have lived with in the world, imitating their lives as their friends and companions.

Prayer: My Lord, who is almighty and full of love, as You showed Your kindness to the woman with the flow of blood, to the blind man and to the paralyzed man by the pool and to many more who You have completely healed form their bodily diseases, please heal me completely from all the weakness of my spirit and from the sins of my body and mind. Make me take on Your image, as You planned. As You continuously nudge me so I find life, also give me the will to persevere in my quest for You and to fully respond to the calls of Your Holy Spirit. To You be the glory forever, Amen.

Chapter 5

A New Creation

Homily 5: The great difference between Christians and men of this world. For the latter, imbued with the spirit of the world, are in heart and mind held by earthly shackles. Christians, however, are possessed by a love for their heavenly Father. They keep Him before their eyes in all their desires.

The true Christians are not sifted like other people

1,2. True Christians have a whole world of difference between them and all other people. They are different in their style of living, their manners, their mind, their speech and their deeds. The rest of the world is one thing and they are another. The children of this world are like wheat in a sieve that is sifted by restless thoughts and the uncertainty of this world. They are constantly tossed to and fro by earthly cares, desires, and their love of material things. Satan tosses such souls as a sifter sifts wheat. Ever since Adam fell, by disobeying God's commandment, and came under the power of darkness, Satan has sifted the whole sinful human race using earthly cares, deceitful thoughts, worries and unjustified agitation. As the wheat in the sieve is continually shaken by the sifter, Satan dashes them relentlessly against the sieve of this earth with many earthly concerns, negative thoughts and anxiety to keep them in bondage to this world. For this reason, the Lord forewarned His apostles about the future attacks of Satan against them; "Satan has sought to sift you as wheat, but I have prayed to My Father so that your faith would not fail" (Lk 22:31-32). This is clear in the life of Cain who became the image of those who had been captured by Satan through their sins as "a fugitive and a vagabond you shall be on the earth" (Gen 4:12). After the children of Adam had violated God's commandment and entered into the state of sin, they acquired a fallen interior nature. They became tossed to and fro relentlessly with continuous thoughts of fear and terror and every sort of disturbance. In the same way, Satan keeps each soul that is not reborn of God tossed by waves of various passions, fears and lusts. As wheat is shaken up constantly in the sieve, so he keeps men's thoughts rattling in all directions. He shakes and entices them by the seductions of this world and by carnal pleasures, fears and agitations. For this reason, Jesus warns us that: "all that is in the world—the lust of the flesh, the lust of the eyes, and the pride of life—is not of the Father but is of the world" (1 Jn 2:16).

 3. The Lord rebuked those who follow the trickeries of Satan and bear the likeness of Cain's evil when he said,

> "You are of your father the devil, and the desires of your father you want to do. He was a murderer

from the beginning, and does not stand in the truth, because there is no truth in him" (Jn 8:44).

In such a way, the whole sinful race of Adam received that condemnation: "a fugitive and a vagabond you shall be on the earth" (Gen 4:12) and so Satan shakes people in the sieve of the earth. For just as from one, Adam, the whole human race was multiplied over the earth, so one corruption of passion entered the entire human race. Thus, Satan became able to sift all of them with continuous vain thoughts. Satan dominated over all those who accepted his authority as a storm which shakes all the plants and as a wave of darkness which spreads at night over all the entire earth. He entices the hearts of all people with the pleasures of the world. He fills every soul that obeys him with a dark ignorance, blindness, and absentmindedness. Only those who have been reborn from above and have been transformed in mind and heart and have moved to another world can escape him, saying "our citizenship is in Heaven" (Phil 3:20). Therefore, they escaped from that condemnation: "There is now no condemnation to those who are in Christ Jesus who do not walk according to the flesh, but according to the Spirit" (Rom 8:1).

Believe that you can be different in order to be truly different
4. The difference between true Christians and the rest of the world is huge. True Christians always have their hearts and minds focused on heavenly matters. Saint Paul clearly explained to us that: "if then you were raised with Christ, seek those things which are above, where Christ is, sitting at the right hand of God" (Col 3:1). Therefore, while they are still in this world, they look at all the goodness of eternal life like looking in a mirror, for

they have received the Holy Spirit and His fellowship that works in them as they are reborn again from the Father. They have received the right to be the children of God in truth and power "as many as received Him, to them He gave the right to become children of God, to those who believe in His name" (Jn 1:12). When they reach an appointed steady stage of freedom, peace and tranquility, Satan is no longer able to sift them with those evil waves of restless thoughts.

Moreover, they are greater than the whole world for they only care for Christ and for the love of the Holy Spirit, as they have "passed from death into life" (Jn 5:24). What distinguishes true Christians from other people is not their external appearance, their use of certain humble words or their style of life and style of clothes, but the true love that Christians have in their hearts for all people and the purity of the thoughts in their minds, as Christ has become the main focus of their lives. Sadly, some Christians are very much like the rest of the world in their hearts and minds. They undergo the same disturbing restlessness and instability of their thoughts. They lack faith and suffer from confusion, agitation and fear as all other people do. They may differ somewhat externally or in their choice of words or their way of acting in certain situations, but in their hearts and minds, they are still shackled by earthly bonds like the rest of the world. They do not have the divine rest and heavenly peace of the Holy Spirit in their hearts because they never earnestly asked God for it, nor did they ever believe that He would stoop down to grant them these wonderful heavenly gifts and free them from all their weakness, fears and anxieties as He said: "if the Son makes you free, you shall be free indeed" (Jn 8:36).

Prayer: O Holy Spirit make me born again in You and free me from the dominion of Satan that he would never again be able to trouble my thoughts, cause me unnecessary anxieties or sift my existence. Jesus, my Lord, since You died for me, Satan has no authority over me. You are my Lord; and my city is where You are. I truly believe that You can change me and form me in Your image. Take away all my weakness, and give me all your strength. For only if You make me free, I shall be free indeed.

The glory of God and the glory of His children
5. The qualities that differentiate true Christians from all other people on the face of the earth are; the renewing of their minds, the tranquility of their thoughts, their genuine love for all people and their earnest desire to be united with God, which is the main objective for which our Lord came to our world. He came to us to give all these heavenly gifts to those who truly believe in Him and desire to be united with Him; as He expressed in His prayer to the Father for us:
> "the glory which You gave Me I have given them, that they may be one just as We are one: I in them, and You in Me; that they may be made perfect in one" (Jn 17:22-23).

Therefore, those Christians possess a glorious, indescribable heavenly richness that comes to them as a result of hard work and endurance in times of temptations and through many trials. All of this can only be attained by the grace of the Holy Spirit. The sight of an earthly king attracts many who wish to see his earthly glory, and everyone with earthly ties desires at least to catch a glimpse of his magnificence, the elegance of his garments or the splendor of his robe, the beauty of his many pearls, the exquisiteness of his crown or the impressive entourage that accompanies him. But spiritual people snub all of these things because they have experienced another heavenly and immaterial glory. They have tasted another unutterable beauty and have participated in other riches. They have received in their inner person another spirit, that is the Holy Spirit.

6. If worldly people so desire the glory of an earthly king, how much more do those the Holy Spirit has touched and whose heart has been pierced by divine love desire the heavenly King. They have been captivated by His beauty and indescribable glory and by the incorruptible glamour and incomprehensible riches of the true and eternal King, Jesus Christ. They are indeed held captive by their genuine desire and longing for Him. Their whole being is pulled completely towards Him. Therefore, the desire of their existence is to obtain these heavenly goods through the Holy Spirit. For the sake of Christ, such Christians regard all earthly beauty, glory, honor, friendship and the riches of royals and friendship with all sorts of authorities as nothing because they have tasted divine beauty; and the life of heavenly immortality has dropped like dew into their souls. Therefore, they passionately long for that love of the heavenly King and there are no other desires before their eyes except for Him. For His sake, they detach themselves from every worldly love and the false promises of those who are in authority and cut themselves loose from every earthly attachment, so that they may always possess that one desire in their hearts. They travel their journey on earth saying:

> "what things were gain to me, these I have counted loss for Christ. Yet indeed I also count all things loss for the excellence of the knowledge of Christ Jesus my Lord, for whom I have suffered the loss of all things, and count them as rubbish, that I may gain Christ and be found in Him, not having my own righteousness, which is from the

law, but that which is through faith in Christ, the righteousness which is from God by faith; that I may know Him and the power of His resurrection, and the fellowship of His sufferings, being conformed to His death, if, by any means, I may attain to the resurrection from the dead" (Phil 3:7-12).

You should already have in your safe box the title deeds for your guaranteed house in heaven
7. The blessed Paul advises us that we all need to obtain this wonderful everlasting life with Christ while we are still in this world: "for we know that if our earthly house, this tent, is destroyed, we have a building from God, a house not made with hands, eternal in the heavens" (2 Cor 5:1). Therefore, all of us need to persevere to attain every virtue and to believe that we can now possess that promised eternal building in heaven as our permanent residence. He also says "if indeed, having been clothed, we shall not be found naked" (2 Cor 5:3), that is being naked without the fellowship of the Holy Spirit in whom alone we find rest. For this reason, the utmost joy of true Christians is when they leave this body and go to that house not made with hands which is guaranteed by the power of the Holy Spirit who dwells in them "who is the guarantee of our inheritance until the redemption of the purchased possession" (Eph 1:14). They fully trust with no fear that when the earthly house of their bodies is destroyed by death, they will move on to the incorruptible heavenly house of the glory of the Holy Spirit who will restore their bodies to the glory of the resurrection, as Saint Paul explained to us:

> "if the Spirit of Him who raised Jesus from the dead dwells in you, He who raised Christ from

> the dead will also give life to your mortal bodies through His Spirit who dwells in you" (Romans 8:11),

"that the life of Jesus also may be manifested in our mortal flesh" and,

> "For we who are in this tent groan, being burdened, not because we want to be unclothed, but further clothed, that mortality may be swallowed up by life" (2 Cor 4:11, 5:4).

The resurrection is our time to blossom into the glory of God by the Holy Spirit who dwells in our bodies

8,9. Let us therefore endeavor, by faith, to excel in every virtue in order to obtain that clothing in this life, so that when we depart from our bodies we will not be found naked as the Holy Spirit has advised us:

> "I counsel you to buy from Me gold refined in the fire, that you may be rich; and white garments, that you may be clothed, that the shame of your nakedness may not be revealed" (Rev 3:18).

For as far as anyone, through faith and genuine desire, has been deemed worthy to receive the Holy Spirit, to that same degree his or her body also will also be glorified in that day. What the soul now stores up within shall then be revealed as a treasure and displayed externally in the heavenly body. They are like the trees that don't show much beauty during the winter but once winter has passed, the warmth of spring makes them blossom and put out leaves, flowers and fruit in a glorious fashion. For all examples of this nature are types and images of Christians at the resurrection. The Sun of Righteousness"(Mal 4:2), Jesus Christ, works in all true Christians to show in them the beauty of the Holy Spirit who clothes them with glory. However, He always remains hidden in their inward parts till the appointed day when He openly reveals to the whole world the glory that God has given them.

In the day of resurrection, by the power of the Sun of Righteousness, the glory of the Holy Spirit will rise up from within, covering the bodies of true Christians to reveal the glory that they had treasured inside their souls during their lives on earth. This is the day in which their bodies will be glorified by means of the light that is currently hidden inside them; this is the power of the Holy Spirit who will then be their clothing, food, drink, exultation, gladness, peace, adornment, and eternal life. For the divine Spirit, who they have been considered worthy to possess, will then bring about in them every beauty of radiance and heavenly splendor. So, we all now can say:

> "our citizenship is in heaven, from which we also eagerly wait for the Savior, the Lord Jesus Christ, who will transform our lowly body that it may be conformed to His glorious body, according to the working by which He is able even to subdue all things to Himself" (Phil 3:20-21).

As Moses body was glorified, so shall our bodies be in the resurrection to new life, but it all begins now

10. Therefore, each one of us ought to believe and press on in our devotion to live a full and upright life. With much hope and endurance, we should acquire the privilege of receiving that heavenly power and the glory of the Holy Spirit inside our souls, so that after our bodies are dissolved, we may receive that beauty which shall clothe and revive us as the apostle says; "If indeed, having being clothed we shall not be found naked" (2 Cor 5:3), and "He shall bring to life our mortal bodies by His

Spirit that dwells in us" (Rom 8:11). For the blessed Moses provided us with a certain example through the glory of the Spirit, which covered his countenance, on which no one could gaze. This example reveals how in the resurrection of the just, the bodies of the saints will be glorified with a glory, which, even now, the souls of saintly and faithful people are deemed worthy to possess, in the inner man. It is written:

> "for we all with unveiled face [that is to say, in the inner man], beholding as in a mirror the glory of the Lord, are being transformed into the same image from glory to glory" (2 Cor 3:18).

Likewise, Moses; "was there with the Lord forty days and forty nights; he neither ate bread nor drank water" (Exod 34:28). It is not possible that a natural body can live without bread for so long, unless he partook of some other spiritual bread. The saints invisibly partake of this bread even now by the power of the Holy Spirit.

Prayer: My Lord, as I am wretched, miserable, poor, blind, and naked, I implore You to clothe me with the glory of Your Holy Spirit who will give eternal life to my mortal body. Please, make me a dwelling place for Your Holy Spirit who will help me to attain all the virtues that You have given me, and will put Your glory on me on the day I will stand in front of You. Please, guide me to live in Your kingdom while I am still on this earth that I may explore my inheritance that You have prepared for me as You promised. You made me in Your image different from all other people, please give me the glory of Your light that You gave to Moses and to all Your saints and give me wings to fly to Your kingdom to peer into the eternal life with You. Permeate my existence now and for all ages to come by the glory of Your Holy Spirit.

11. In these two examples, the blessed Moses

shows us what glory true Christians will receive at the resurrection; namely, the glory of light and the spiritual delights of the Holy Spirit which they are deemed worthy to possess even now in a hidden manner. Because of this, these gifts of the Spirit will also be glorified in their bodies then. The saints possess this glory in their souls even now, as was said above, but then it will cover and clothe their naked bodies. It will sweep them up into Heaven and they will at last come to rest, both body and soul, with the Lord forever. When God created Adam, He did not furnish him with material wings as birds have, but He prepared for him the wings of the Holy Spirit to give him a taste of heaven. He will give him these wings at the resurrection, to lift him and direct him wherever the Spirit wishes. The saints are now already deemed worthy to possess these wings to fly up in their minds to the realm of heavenly thoughts.

It is now clear that Christians live in another world, eat from another table, are clothed in a different style, and prefer different enjoyment, different conversations, and a different mentality. They are already considered worthy to have the power of the Holy Spirit in their souls. Because of this they exceed all other people. Therefore, their bodies will also be worthy to receive eternal blessings in the resurrection. They will be permeated with the glory of the Holy Spirit that their souls in this life have already experienced.

Let us march onwards to heaven

12. Therefore, each one of us should strive, making every effort to pursue all virtues diligently. We ought to believe and seek from the Lord that glory of the inner man, that we may participate in the holiness of the Spirit so that, purged from the lust of evil, we may receive in the resurrection the glory that will clothe our bodies,

otherwise we would be found naked. This will cover any deformity and will revive and transform our bodies in the heavenly kingdom forever. Christ will descend from Heaven and raise up all the generations that have fallen asleep from the beginning of time, as the holy Scripture demonstrates:

> "I do not want you to be ignorant, brethren, concerning those who have fallen asleep, lest you sorrow as others who have no hope. For if we believe that Jesus died and rose again, even so God will bring with Him those who sleep in Jesus. For this we say to you by the word of the Lord, that we who are alive and remain until the coming of the Lord will by no means precede those who are asleep. For the Lord Himself will descend from heaven with a shout, with the voice of an archangel, and with the trumpet of God. And the dead in Christ will rise first. Then we who are alive and remain shall be caught up together with them in the clouds to meet the Lord in the air. And thus, we shall always be with the Lord" (1 Thes 4:13-17)

who will divide the whole world into two groups. He will call to Himself those who bear His seal, that is, the sign of the Spirit as they are His very own and He will place them at His right hand. He says; "My sheep hear My voice and I know My own and I am known by Mine" (Jn 10:27, 14).

Then their bodies shall be wrapped in divine glory because of their good works. They themselves will be filled with the glory of the Spirit that they enjoyed in their souls in this life. So they will be illuminated by divine light and caught up into heaven "to meet the Lord in the air. And thus we shall be always with the Lord" (1 Thes 4:17), reigning with Him forever and ever. Amen.

Chapter 6

Harmony Between the Holy Spirit and Our Free Will

Homily 9: The promises of God to each one of us are fulfilled after various tests of our free will. This allows us to demonstrate our genuine desire to cling to God alone.

The Holy Spirit works with our will in a long-term plan

1-7. The Holy Spirit works with our soul in a mystical way while the individual patiently uses the opportunities that come his or her way to prove that he or she truly desires God. The grace of God works perfectly in those who have demonstrated over time that they have freely chosen to please the Holy Spirit by putting aside all the world's passing pleasures and false promises.

There are many examples of this in the Bible. Joseph rejected the opportunity to sin with his master's wife. Instead he accepted imprisonment and dishonor, then later he was found to be upright in the sight of God who made him a leader over the whole of Egypt (Gen 39-41). The same happened to David. Though God anointed him king by the hand of Samuel the prophet, he was dreadfully afflicted and had to flee into the desert because of Saul's plots to kill him. Though he was the one who God anointed to be king, he suffered many afflictions. But, after he had patiently endured everything, placing all his trust in God alone, God's promise to him was finally fulfilled. The same also happened to Moses. God arranged for him to become the son of Pharaoh's daughter and to grow up as a leader "in all the wisdom of the Egyptians" and to be "mighty in words and deeds" (Acts 7:22), but only when he rejected all of these things;

> "choosing rather to suffer affliction with the people of God than to enjoy the passing pleasures of sin, esteeming the reproach of Christ greater riches than the treasures in Egypt" (Heb 11:25-26),

then God made him a savior for his people and like "a god for Pharaoh" (Exod 7:1). You can also consider what happened to Abraham. How long did he wait before God promised to give him a son? When he fully believed that "what He had promised He was also able to perform" (Rom 4:21), he was found faithful and obtained the promise after he endured trials and temptations for many years. Noah also patiently waited for a hundred years before he saw God's promise come true, yet he never doubted for a moment that God would do what He had said. "Here is the patience of the saints; here are those who keep the commandments of God and the faith of Jesus" (Rev 14:12).

All these examples from the Holy Scripture show us that the power of the Holy Spirit (which is given to

faithful souls) comes with much endurance and patience in trials and in testing circumstances. Our free will is put to the test by all sorts of afflictions. And when we "do not grieve the Holy Spirit of God" (Eph 4:30) in any way but work in harmony with the grace of God by keeping all God's commandments, then God considers us worthy to be freed from evil desires. Jesus said, "therefore if the Son makes you free, you shall be free indeed" (Jn 8:36). We also receive, full adoption by the Spirit, which is a true mystery, along with spiritual riches and wisdom which are not of this world. For this reason, such people differ in all things from other people who have the spirit of this world. They cry out joyfully saying:
"Now we have received, not the spirit of the world, but the Spirit who is from God, that we might know the things that have been freely given to us by God" (1 Cor 2:12).

Prayer: My God and Savior, give me the power, wisdom and watchfulness to refuse to obey the power of darkness even for a second or give in even for a centimeter. Work with me as You did with Noah, Joseph, David, Moses and Abraham. Help me to show you, through You, that I have chosen You with my own free will over anything else in this world, waiting patiently to be filled with Your Holy Spirit like the five wise virgins. Please, help me to be triumphant in times of tribulations and trials and to endure till I receive your crown of life.

The fire of heavenly love is the gift of the Holy Spirit
8-10. Indeed, a person like this who is filled with the Holy Spirit "judges all things, yet he himself is rightly judged by no one" (1 Cor 2:15) as he or she is fully aware of his or her own thoughts and motivations. But no one from the world can size up this person's depth

or judge him or her. Only a person who has the same heavenly Spirit can know one who is like him or her, as the apostle says:

> "These things we also speak, not in words which man's wisdom teaches but which the Holy Spirit teaches, comparing spiritual things with spiritual. But the natural man does not receive the things of the Spirit of God, for they are foolishness to him; nor can he know them, because they are spiritually discerned. But he who is spiritual judges all things, yet he himself is rightly judged by no one" (1 Cor 2:13-15).

Such a person despises all the things the world considers to be precious, such as riches, luxury, sensual pleasures, and even worldly knowledge. Saint Paul said:

> "what things were gain to me, these I have counted loss for Christ. Yet indeed I also count all things loss for the excellence of the knowledge of Christ Jesus my Lord, for whom I have suffered the loss of all things, and count them as rubbish, that I may gain Christ" (Phil 3:7-8).

Just as a man suffering from a fever will reject any food or drink that is offered to him even if it is very deliciously tempting, because of the hot fever, so those who long for the Holy Spirit are lovesick for God. They burn with a divine and heavenly fire which the Lord came to earth to kindle, as he said "I came to send fire on the earth, and how I wish it were already kindled!" (Lk 12:49). As the love of Christ is kindled in their hearts, they despise everything that is offered by this world. Nothing that comes from the earth can sway them from such a great love, as the apostle Paul explained that nothing can "separate us from the love of Christ" (Rom 8:35). Therefore, people cannot immerse themselves in the love of the Holy Spirit unless they cut themselves off from everything that ties them to the world and surrender themselves fully to the love of Christ. So, no desire for power, glory, honor, worldly friendships or anything else can distract them from the main aim of their lives. They concentrate totally on caring for their spirits and intellects, waiting in hope for the coming of the Holy Spirit. The Lord speaks in a similar way: "by your patience possess your souls" (Lk 21:19). And again, He says, "seek first the kingdom of God and His righteousness, and all these things shall be added to you" (Mt 6:33).

We renounce all other things to be joined to Him in spirit

11. Everyone who really strives to be joined to God, persevering in prayer in obedience to God's word and His commandments, will be able to escape from the darkness of evil powers. For the mind that never ceases to scrutinize itself and to seek the Lord can preserve its soul by always obeying the Lord and by clinging only to Him; "bringing every thought into captivity to the obedience of Christ" (2 Cor 10:5, 9-10). For Jesus said,

> "I am the vine, you are the branches. He who abides in Me, and I in him, bears much fruit. As the Father loved Me, I also have loved you; abide in My love. If you keep My commandments, you will abide in My love, just as I have kept My Father's commandments and abide in His love" (Jn 15:5).

The gift of the grace of Christ finds its place in the soul that has abided in Christ preparing itself to receive the Holy Spirit by striving to keep all His commandments. This eager soul ensures the mind has not "insulted the Spirit of grace" (Heb 10:29) through any selfish ambition, pride, love of the world, love of honor, desire for position, selfish opinions, worldly desires or association with evil men.

Prayer: My Lord, help me to reject every worldly object and earthly concept of praise, pride, honor or power for the love of knowing You. I cannot do that on my own, but if You free me, I will be free indeed. Please, give me Your true freedom and untie me from all the worldly connections that separate me from You, so that I unite with You in one spirit. I am waiting for the fire of Your Holy Spirit to kindle the fire of Your love in me.

Love your God with all your heart

12,13. For how lovely it is when a spiritual person devotes himself or herself totally to the Lord and clings to Him alone, always walking in His commands without getting weary till he or she becomes united with Him in one spirit, just as the apostle says "he who is joined to the Lord is one spirit with Him" (1 Cor 6:17). But if people give themselves over to the cares of this world, or to false glory or high positions, or to human honors or worldly thoughts, they will be unable to flee from the bondage of this world, or to get rid of the dark passions in which they are held captive by the powers of the devil. The reason is that they love and do the will of the dark powers and they have not totally despised the pursuit of evil.

Therefore, to obtain the promise of His Holy Spirit: let us prepare ourselves so that we may come to the Lord with a perfect willingness and a firm intention to always follow Him; and let us rekindle our love for Christ doing His will and fulfilling His commandments; let us separate ourselves completely from any attachment to this world and instead hold fast to Him alone with all our souls; let us keep Him alone before our eyes as our focus and aim; let us steady our mind from swerving away from the love of the Lord and from eagerly seeking Him; let us follow the straight path of justice and always scrutinize ourselves.

Through His grace we will be freed from the destructive power of the dark desires, which attack our souls, so that we may be considered worthy to enter the eternal kingdom to enjoy Christ forever. Glory to the Father and the Son and the Holy Spirit, perfect Trinity, for all ages. Amen.

Chapter 7

Our Unity with the Holy Spirit

Homily 10: The grace of the Holy Spirit is attained through humility and diligence but is squandered through arrogance and laziness.

True love for Jesus Christ
    1,2. Those who love Jesus in truth and long to be united with Him in full hope and strong faith don't need anyone to remind or encourage them. They cannot bear to be separated from Christ even for a moment because of their tender love for Him and their strong desire to be one with Him. For they are fully nailed with Him to His cross and they feel their growing desire for His heavenly wedding. Having been stricken by His love and having a strong yearning for His righteousness, their craving to be illuminated by the Holy Spirit never diminishes as they cry out:
> "I have been crucified with Christ; it is no longer I who live, but Christ lives in me; and the life which I now live in the flesh I live by faith in the Son of

God, who loved me and gave Himself for me" (Gal 2:20).

Being convinced in their mind that; "those who are Christ's have crucified the flesh with its passions and desires" (Gal 5:24), they are afraid to do anything that might separate them from Him.

Taken by force and diligence but lost by laziness and carelessness

When they are granted, through faith, the understanding of divine mysteries and partnership in heavenly pleasures, they remain on guard, as they never put their trust in themselves but put all their trust in the Lord who said "without Me you can do nothing" (Jn 15:5). They do not think much of themselves as they always keep in mind what David said: "Lord, my heart is not haughty, nor my eyes lofty. Neither do I concern myself with great matters, nor with things too profound for me" (Ps 131:1). The more they receive from the Holy Spirit, the more diligent they become in their quest for heaven. The more riches they receive, the more convinced they are that they are the poorest of all God's children. The more they progress in their spiritual journey, the more thirsty and hungry they are for partnership with the Holy Spirit. Therefore, they always want more heavenly joy as is mentioned in the book of the wisdom of Ben Sirach:

> "Come to Me, you who desire Me, and take your fill of My fruits. For the remembrance of Me is sweeter than honey, and My inheritance is sweeter than the honeycomb. Those who eat Me will hunger for more, and those who drink Me will thirst for more" (Sirach 24:19-21).

Those who pursue the Lord with such passion are

worthy of His eternal life and worthy to be freed from all lusts and to obtain the fullness of the grace of the hidden and mystical communion with the Holy Spirit.

3. There are other people who through laziness and carelessness lose their chance to be freed from all the lusts of the flesh. As they never expected or even hoped for true partnership with the Holy Spirit, they only wanted partial freedom from slavery to the desires of this world. Once they have had some spiritual pleasure, they believe that they have achieved it all. As they become arrogant, they neglect prayers and Bible reading, which later leads to their fall from grace. Therefore, Saint Paul advised us:

> "each one of you show the same diligence to the full assurance of hope until the end, that you do not become sluggish, but imitate those who through faith and patience inherit the promises" (Heb 6:11-12).

4. Those who truly love Christ never think much of themselves even if they have done thousands of good deeds. When they have fasted, spent long periods praying, given their time for the service of God and provided for the poor, they feel they have only started their journey towards righteousness. As their love is never quenched, they long for Him all day long with prayers that fuel their thirst and hunger to fulfil all His commandments, as if they were love-struck. And so, the Holy Spirit guides them into complete fellowship with the Son of God for the righteousness of their souls. As the Holy Spirit removes the veil from their souls, they stare face to face into the Lord to be filled with His heavenly light, hoping to be united with Him in the likeness of His death. As they become confident that they will receive the power of the Holy Spirit that will free them

completely from all the lust of the body, the weakness of the spirit and the desires of the world, they confirm what Saint Paul said:

> "We all, with unveiled face, beholding as in a mirror the glory of the Lord, are being transformed into the same image from glory to glory, just as by the Spirit of the Lord" (2 Cor 3:18).

When they are fully washed with His blood in body and soul, the Lord will then give them the right to be a dwelling place for the Holy Spirit who qualifies them for eternal life.

We must through many tribulations enter the Kingdom
5. The faithful soul cannot attain all of this grace without many tribulations and trials. Through various trials, suffering and tribulations, the soul grows in grace and attains fellowship with the Holy Spirit. When a person endures all the evil trials with courage and patience, the soul reaches a full, fearless state and qualifies for all heavenly honor and spiritual gifts.

> "Blessed is the man who endures temptation; for when he has been approved, he will receive the crown of life which the Lord has promised to those who love Him" (Jm 1:12).

True Christians know that "We must through many tribulations enter the kingdom of God" (Acts 14:22). But they always encourage themselves saying; "Who shall separate us from the love of Christ? Shall tribulation, or distress, or persecution, or famine, or nakedness, or peril, or sword?" (Rom 8:35). This is the way we become heirs of the kingdom of our Lord Jesus Christ.

Chapter 8

The Seal

Homily 12: Comparison between the state of Adam before he transgressed the commandment of God and his state after he lost his natural and heavenly image.

Adam lost his pure nature and heavenly image

1,2. When Adam broke the commandment of God, he lost two essential things: the pure heavenly nature that God created him with; and the image of God that was placed on him at his creation in order for him to reach the kingdom of heaven.

Adam was like a very valuable coin, made from pure gold, with the image of the sovereign King engraved on it. But, when he fell, the image of the King faded away and the nature of the coin changed into a cheap, fake metal. So, the coin lost its value and became good for nothing. That is what happened to Adam when he entertained evil intentions and allowed bad thoughts to develop in his mind. He then lost God. Though Adam remained a living being (1 Cor 15:45), he was dead to

God who looks into the minds and hearts of His creation. As good Christians turn their eyes away from evil scenes, God turns his eyes away from those who do evil.

6-10. Adam possessed everything and had fellowship with God before he fell from grace. The Word, the Logos, taught him everything, so that he was able to name all things. He was covered with the glory of the Holy Spirit so that he and Eve did not know they were "naked" (Gen 2:25). Nevertheless, after they disobeyed the command, they then saw themselves as naked and they were covered with shame. The Word Himself was with Adam and was everything to him; knowledge, experience, inheritance, teaching, covering and glory. For John says, "in the beginning was the Word" (Jn 1: 1). Before Adam and Eve sinned, they were covered with God's glory, which took the place of clothing. Just as the Spirit worked in the prophets, instructed them, dwelled within them and appeared outwardly to them, so He also did with Adam. The Spirit was with him and taught him, saying; "Give this a name, call it such and such". Though the Word was everything to Adam, he still transgressed against God's commandments. Let us stress that even those who are filled with the Holy Spirit can experience natural thoughts because they possess free will, which enables them to consent to good or to evil. So also, Adam, even when he was with God in Paradise, broke God's commandment of his own free will and obeyed his darker thoughts by his own choice. However even after he fell, Adam still had knowledge of God, but like a robber who is brought in front of a court, he knew his wrongdoing. Likewise, the fornicator knows that he or she is doing wrong. Do not people know that God exists even without knowing the Bible, simply by calling on their natural reason? For God speaks to them in many ways, saying:

"Do you not know that God exists who rules all creatures?" Even the demons cried out saying; "What do I have to do with You, Jesus, You Son of God? Have You come here to torment us before the time?" (Mt 8:29)

The fall of Adam brought him the knowledge of good and evil. He was created in the image of God, possessing honor and purity, but when he fell, he was cast out of Paradise and experienced the effect of evil on himself. Let us therefore, as skilled merchants, work to possess the heavenly inheritance. Let us learn to lay hold of the good things God gives us that will always remain with us.

Poor in spirit but making many rich
3. Jesus said, "blessed are the poor in spirit, for theirs is the kingdom of heaven" (Mt 5:3). One might ask how someone who has progressed towards the knowledge of God could be poor in spirit. Actually, until a person acquires the perfect knowledge of God, he or she remains poor in spirit. Then when people make progress and arrive at this understanding, grace itself teaches them that they are God's chosen people. So, they never think of themselves as important, but maintain a lowly and humble attitude, as if they had nothing, even though they have all knowledge and riches. Saint Paul said about these people that they live "as poor, yet making many rich; as having nothing, and yet possessing all things" (2 Cor 6:10). Those who are poor in spirit do not consider themselves to be worthy of anything, just as Abraham still called himself dust and ashes (Gen 18:27) when he was God's chosen one, and David, the anointed King, said: "But I am a worm, and no man; a reproach of men and despised by the people" (Ps 22:6).

Partaking of Christ's sufferings
4,5. Those who wish to be co-heirs with Abraham, David and all the other citizens of the heavenly city ought to obtain the same humility of spirit and not regard themselves as anything in themselves. For although grace works in individual Christians in different ways, yet they all belong to the same nation, having the same mind and speaking with one tongue. They recognize one another as Saint Paul taught us saying: "For as the body is one and has many members, but all the members of that one body, being many, are one body, so also is Christ" (1 Cor 12:12).

All the righteous people had to go through many tribulations in their journey on the narrow road. The apostle says "to the present hour we both hunger and thirst, and we are poorly clothed, and beaten, and homeless" (1 Cor 4:11). Moreover, the Lord Himself suffered many tribulations and lived on this earth as though He had forgotten His divine glory, making Himself an example for us to imitate:

> "But when you do good and suffer, if you take it patiently, this is commendable before God. For to this you were called, because Christ also suffered for us, leaving us an example, that you should follow His steps" (1 Pet 2:20-21).

The apostles indeed followed the example of Christ in His suffering, therefore the apostle also says through the Holy Spirit, "imitate me, just as I also imitate Christ" (1 Cor 11:1). But if you seek the glory of men and worldly honor and desire the fleshly pleasures, you have swerved from the right way, especially as the Lord says "how can you believe, who receive honor from one another, and do not seek the honor that comes from the only God?" (Jn 5:44). You should be crucified with

Him who was crucified for you and suffer with Him who suffered for you, so that you can be glorified with Him who is always glorified.

> "I have been crucified with Christ; it is no longer I who live, but Christ lives in me; and the life which I now live in the flesh I live by faith in the Son of God, who loved me and gave Himself for me" (Gal 2:20).

There is no possible way except the narrow road of suffering by which we can enter the city of the saints where we find our rest and reign there with the King of kings forever and ever. This why Saint Peter advised us saying:

> "Beloved, do not think it strange concerning the fiery trial which is to try you, as though some strange thing happened to you; but rejoice to the extent that you partake of Christ's sufferings, that when His glory is revealed, you may also be glad with exceeding joy" (1 Pet 4:12-13).

"Therefore, since Christ suffered for us in the flesh, arm yourselves also with the same mind" (1 Pet 4:1).

Prayer: My Lord, please take away my deep-seated arrogance and self-importance that is promoted by my ego and instead give me the true humility that You have demonstrated in Your life on earth. Help me to shy away from all positions of authority and move away from the first seat in an honorable place and accept the last seat where I can meet You. If this is my cross, please make it the narrow way that leads me to my resurrection in my new nature to inherit Your promised kingdom with You.

We cannot search the mind of God, we can only submit to His will

11,12. We cannot search the mind of God or reach Him through intellectual understanding. For the more you wish to search and approach God using human knowledge, the more deeply you fall away from Him and you end up understanding nothing. You can only receive Him through those mysterious and incomprehensible visits of God to you that happen each day. If you already find it difficult to fully know your own soul, comprehend your own thoughts, understand the true motives of your own desires and assess your personality and its characteristics, how can you scrutinize the thoughts of God and know His very mind? As you go to the river's shore and drink as much as you need and continue on your way, not worrying about the river's source or how it flows and similarly as you like to have your skin tanned in the summer, not investigating how much light the sun contains or how high it ascends, you should take whatever God gives you for your benefit without asking many questions. If then, you seek the Lord in the depths, there you will find Him doing wonders (Exod 15:11) inside you. If you seek Him in caves, there you will find Him in the midst of the lions, guarding Daniel (Dan 6:10-23). If you seek Him in fire, there you will find Him, the source of help to His three faithful servants (Dan 3). If you seek Him on a mountain, there you will discover Him with Elijah and Moses (Mt 17). He is, therefore, everywhere, both under the earth and above the heavens and also dwelling in us. He is everywhere.

Whoever possesses the seal of God will be recognized by Him on the last day

13,14. In the last day, God will know His people as they too will know Him. As He said "I am the good shepherd; and I know My sheep, and am known by My own" (Jn 10:14). He will separate them from the rest of the world. As He said:

> "When the Son of Man comes in His glory, and all the holy angels with Him, then He will sit on the throne of His glory. All the nations will be gathered before Him, and He will separate them one from another, as a shepherd divides his sheep from the goats. And He will set the sheep on His right hand, but the goats on the left. Then the King will say to those on His right hand, 'Come, you blessed of My Father, inherit the kingdom prepared for you from the foundation of the world'... Then He will also say to those on the left hand, 'Depart from Me, you cursed, into the everlasting fire prepared for the devil and his angels'... And these will go away into everlasting punishment, but the righteous into eternal life" (Mt 25:31-46).

He will know them by His seal on them, as John saw in his revelation "we have sealed the servants of our God on their foreheads" (Rev 7:3). Saint John also describes the symbolic number of those who were sealed:

> "I heard the number of those who were sealed. One hundred and forty-four thousands of all the tribes of the children of Israel were sealed. After these things I looked, and behold, a great multitude which no one could number, of all

nations, tribes, peoples, and tongues, standing before the throne and before the Lamb, clothed with white robes, with palm branches in their hands" (Rev 7:4,9).

In the day of judgment, when "the severity of God" (Rom 11:22) is shown, and all the tribes of the earth are gathered together, the good Shepherd will summon His flock, then whoever possesses the seal of God will be recognized by Him, and He will gather them together from all the nations as "He calls his own sheep by name and leads them out" (Jn 10:3). Those who belong to Him will follow Him when they hear His voice. He will divide the world into two flocks. One flock is full of darkness and this group will depart to the eternal fire. The other flock is full of light and will be led to eternal life into heaven, which becomes its inheritance. You need to know that whatever we now have in our souls will later shine in splendor. This will be shown to all and will clothe our bodies with glory. It is just like roots which are now covered with soil, but then produce their fruits, flowers and beauty in the spring. The good roots become apparent as well as those that have thorns. Likewise, in the day of judgment, everyone will show openly what they did when they were in their bodies. Both the evil deeds and the good ones will be manifest. For there will indeed be a universal judgment and retribution. This glory of God now shines splendidly from the hearts of Christians. At the resurrection, their bodies will be covered with another garment as they rise, one that is divine. They will be nourished with the heavenly food that nourished Moses for forty days and forty nights on the mountain of Sinai. As Saint Paul taught us:

"How are the dead raised up? And with what body do they come? Foolish one, what you sow is not made alive unless it dies. And what you sow, you do not sow that body that shall be, but mere grain—perhaps wheat or some other grain. But God gives it a body as He pleases, and to each seed its own body.... There are also celestial bodies and terrestrial bodies; but the glory of the celestial is one, and the glory of the terrestrial is another. There is one glory of the sun, another glory of the moon, and another glory of the stars; for one star differs from another star in glory. So also, is the resurrection of the dead. The body is sown in corruption, it is raised in incorruption. It is sown in dishonor, it is raised in glory. It is sown in weakness, it is raised in power. It is sown a natural body, it is raised a spiritual body. There is a natural body, and there is a spiritual body. And so it is written, "The first man Adam became a living being." The last Adam became a life-giving spirit. However, the spiritual is not first, but the natural, and afterward the spiritual. The first man was of the earth, made of dust; the second Man is the Lord from heaven. As was the man of dust, so also are those who are made of dust; and as is the heavenly Man, so also are those who are heavenly. And as we have borne the image of the man of dust, we shall also bear the image of the heavenly Man" (1 Cor 15:35-49).

Prayer: My Lord and Savior, fill me and all my existence with the glory of Your Holy Spirit that will be changed into glorious heavenly white clothing, which will cover me in heaven so that I will not be naked. Though I now bear the image of the earthly man of dust, when I die give me the image of Your heavenly glory by Your Holy

Spirit. O what a wonderful day it will be when the sting of death is no more and when I see Your face through Your mercy.

His Spirit gives mysterious power and understanding to the souls of those who truly love Him

15-18. The Spirit gives us the story of Martha and her sister Mary.

> "Now it happened as they went that He entered a certain village; and a certain woman named Martha welcomed Him into her house. And she had a sister called Mary, who also sat at Jesus' feet and heard His word. But Martha was distracted with much serving, and she approached Him and said, 'Lord, do You not care that my sister has left me to serve alone? Therefore, tell her to help me.' And Jesus answered and said to her, 'Martha, Martha, you are worried and troubled about many things. But one thing is needed, and Mary has chosen that good part, which will not be taken away from her'" (Lk 10:38-42).

Martha basically complained to the Lord about Mary saying: "I am busy with many things, so how can she sit here at Your feet?" But, the Lord explained that Mary had left everything to sit at His feet. For when anyone loves Jesus and really gives himself or herself to Him attentively and not in a superficial way, persevering in love, God is already planning to reward that soul for that love. This happens even though people do not know what they are about to receive or what portion God is about to bestow on them. Indeed, when Mary loved Jesus and sat at His feet, Jesus gave her a certain hidden power from His very own being. For the words which God spoke to Mary in peace contained a certain power. And these words penetrated her heart and brought His soul to her soul, His Spirit to her spirit and a divine power filled her heart. That power remained there as a possession which cannot be taken away. For this reason, the Lord, who knew what He had given to Mary, said, "Mary has chosen that good part, which will not be taken away from her" (Lk 10:42).

But shortly afterwards, the works of service that Martha kindly did brought her also that gift of grace. She also received the same divine power in her soul.

When the Lord spoke with Mary, power went out of Him as the Holy Spirit mingled with her soul. The same happened with Zacchaeus, the sinful woman who let her hair down and wiped the feet of the Lord, the Samaritan woman and the good thief. Now those who pursue God in love, having abandoned everything else and persevered in prayers, are secretly taught things they have never known before. For truth comes to those who desire it and it teaches them, as Jesus said: I am the truth (Jn 14:6). The Truth in person shows Himself to be faithful. Therefore, whoever dedicates himself or herself to various forms of service and eagerly performs these activities motivated by zeal, faith and the love of God will be led by that service to the knowledge of truth itself. For the Lord appears to their souls and teaches them how the Holy Spirit operates. He causes man to walk in the fellowship of the Holy Spirit.

Prayer: My Lord, You are the working and loving Word of God, the Logos. Look at me and change me by Your true word. Give me all the understanding I need and the power I lack and the love I desire. As You worked in all your saints and formed them in Your image, please work in me and form me in Your image.

Glory and adoration to the Father and the Son and the Holy Spirit forever. Amen.

Chapter 9

Illumination for the Eyes of Our Hearts

Homily 14: Those who turn their thoughts and minds over to God, look forward to having the eyes of their hearts illuminated. Therefore, God sanctifies them and deems them worthy to receive His mysteries. In this homily, we learn what we ought to do to obtain the good things of heaven. We also learn about the land of Satan and the land of the angels and that both are impalpable and invisible.

The enlightenment of the eyes of our hearts is the aim of all our prayers

1-3. Everything that people do is done for a motive. Unless a person is fully convinced of the purpose of his labor and is confident that there will be a profit, he does not see any point in his labor. The farmer sows his seeds and toils the soil in the hope of a good crop as Saint Paul says, "he who ploughs should ploughs in hope" (1 Cor 9:10). Every enthusiastic trader works very hard in expectation of a profit. So also, in the kingdom of heaven, individuals put their lives fully in the Lord's hands, persevering in prayers and supplications, giving up all the lusts and desires of this world in the hope that God will illuminate the eyes of their hearts. Saint Paul prayed that Christians would experience this, saying:

> "the eyes of your understanding (heart) being enlightened; that you may know what is the hope of His calling, what are the riches of the glory of His inheritance in the saints" (Eph 1:18).

People in the kingdom of heaven wait for the Lord to come to them and show Himself to them as He promised, saying "I will love him and manifest Myself to him" (Jn 14:21). The Lord cleanses them from sin that dwells inside them. But they must not rely on their own labors, as the Lord comes and lives in them through the perfect work of the Holy Spirit. When they have tasted the goodness of the Lord and experienced the fruit of the Spirit, then the veil of darkness is lifted and the light of Christ shines splendidly, bringing unspeakable joy. Then, they will be completely satisfied, full of love for the Lord, having more joy than a merchant who rejoices in a large profit. However, they must always be careful to ensure that the evil, wicked spirits do not steal their joy or the fruit of their work before they obtain the heavenly kingdom, which is the new Jerusalem that comes down from heaven (Rev 21:2).

Therefore, let us ask God to take off from us the old man (the old nature) and afterwards put on us the new man, who is our Lord Jesus Christ who came to us from heaven, so that He will lead us to the greatest tranquility and joy. For the Lord, who wishes to fill us with a taste of the kingdom, says "without Me you can do nothing" (Jn 15:5). God worked through the apostles, using them to enlighten many others. They taught them to become brothers, sisters and children of Christ (Mt 12:50) and to live in an outstanding way so that their hearts and minds would be set apart for God. For when people surrender to God their secret possessions, that is, their minds and thoughts, not occupying themselves with any other matter, thoughts or distractions, the Lord shares with them His mysteries as He said "I have called you friends, for all things that I heard from My Father I have made known to you" (Jn 15:15). He also gives them from His holiness and purity, thus providing them with heavenly food and spiritual drink (1 Cor 10:4).

Prayer: My heavenly Father who feeds me on the food of heaven, please enlighten the eyes of my heart that I can see You and see my way to Your land. Remove the veil from my heart and soul that I may never again get distracted with those little things of this world that stop me from being fully united with You. Though I am blind, I look forward in hope and with full confidence to that day when I say: I was blind and now I can see.

True Christians live by the Holy Spirit

4,5. Take the example of a very rich man who has children and servants. Surely, the food he offers his servants will be different from the food he feeds his own children. The children are heirs of their father and they eat with him for they are like him. So also, Christ, the true Lord, has created all things and nourishes both evil and good people. As He fathers his children "who were born, not of blood, nor of the will of the flesh, nor of the will of man, but of God" (Jn 1:13), He gives them His grace. So, the Lord nourishes them with special food and drink, which He does not give to the others. He gives them Himself, as He says "he who eats My flesh and drinks My blood abides in Me, and I in him" (Jn 6:56). Therefore, the apostle says "we are members of His body, of His flesh and of His bones" (Eph 5:30). Those who possess this true inheritance have been fathered as sons of the heavenly Father and they dwell in their Father's house, as the Lord says "a slave does not abide in the house forever, but a son abides forever" (Jn 8:35). Therefore, if we wish to also be begotten by our heavenly Father, we ought to act in a way that sets us apart from other people; showing zeal, effort and diligence, loving others, speaking well in our conversations and living in faith and in the fear of God. We need to seek God as our only inheritance, as David said: "the Lord is the portion of my inheritance and my cup" (Ps 16:5). Thus, when the Lord sees our good intentions and our steadfastness, He demonstrates His mercy to us and cleanses us by the heavenly Word of God.

The land of God is our habitat
6,7. There is a habitat for cattle, a habitat for birds and another for fish. If the birds wanted to live in the habitat of cattle, they would be easily caught by hunters. Each creature finds rest, safety and nourishment in its natural habitat. Also, Satan has his own homeland where the powers of darkness and the spirits of evil dwell and walk about and find their rest. Likewise, there is a land of God where the camp of saints is. Armies of holy angels walk about and find their rest there. Neither the world of darkness nor the world of God can be seen by human eyes or touched by human senses. But only those who are spiritual can see the world of Satan and the world of divine light with the eyes of their hearts. Christians are like the birds. They only find their rest, safety and nourishment in the land of God who feeds them with heavenly food. But, if they move to the land of the power of darkness, they risk their safety and their eternal inheritance. Therefore, we should zealously make sure

that we have been sown in that invisible land of God and planted in the heavenly vineyard.

    Glory to Him for all eternity for His mercies. Amen.

Chapter 10

A Personal Invitation to the Kingdom

Homily 16: Spiritual people face many troubles and temptations that spring from hidden sin which is deep seated in their hearts.

We were created good and pure with no evil in us

1,2. God created all intellectual creatures such as humans, angels and even the devil so that they would be good, simple and pure. God never created anything that is bad or inherently evil. For after He completed all of His creation; "God saw everything that He had made, and indeed it was very good" (Gen 1:31). People who believe that evil was created to be evil are ignorant. Those who turned to evil chose to do so of their own free will; by their own free will they chose to deviate away from God's purpose. If we say that God created them evil, we would be falsely labelling God, who shall judge everyone according to his deeds, as unjust. Though the evil power tries to have influence over us, it does not compose any part of our existence. The presence of evil power in our life is not like wine and water mixed together to form a new mixed nature, but it is like wheat and weeds growing together separately in the same field (Mt 13:24-30). In a well, you can see clear water despite layers of mud settled in the bottom, but if the water is stirred up it all looks muddy again. The souls of those whose desires are stirred by Satan and become defiled by him are also like this. Moreover, they become united with him as two united spirits, joining together in the pursuit of evil deeds; for that reason, the Bible declares to us, "he who is joined to a harlot is one body with her" and "for 'the two,' He says, 'shall become one flesh'" (1 Cor 6:16). On the other hand, the unity of the soul with the Holy Spirit is like the union between a husband and wife; though they could be in different places, they are still one as Saint Paul taught us, "he who is joined to the Lord is one spirit with Him" (1 Cor 6:17).

The Sun of Righteousness heals all our weakness

3,4. Those who are wise and have years of experience with the Holy Spirit fully understand that the evil powers try to work in them to move them away from the path of salvation. They are like a farmer with many years of experience who knows how to enjoy the times of plenty and how to endure the times of need. He is naturally careful in good times and hopeful in difficult times. Those who have only just tasted the sweetness of their relationship with God panic if they occasionally feel that the grace of God does not fully support them. But the ones who have a strong and deep relationship with the Holy Spirit and are rich in grace, know how to wait for the mercy of God in difficult times, when they do not feel God's support. Therefore, in times of trouble they do not fall into despair. They call on God who certainly supports them, for He fully understands their needs and knows their thoughts. This is well portrayed by David saying:

> "O Lord, You have searched me and known me. You know my sitting down and my rising up; You understand my thought afar off. You comprehend my path and my lying down and are acquainted with all my ways. For there is not a word on my tongue, but behold, O Lord, You know it altogether. You have hedged me behind and before and laid your hand upon me. Such knowledge is too wonderful for me; it is high, I cannot attain it" (Ps 139: 1-6).

The souls of men are like a land full of muddy puddles but when the sun shines, it warms it up and turns it into dry clean land. Similarly, when the Sun of Righteousness shines on the children of God to heal them, they are filled with the Holy Spirit who takes away all their fears and bad desires and makes them rich in grace. "The Sun of Righteousness shall arise with healing in His wings; and you shall go out and grow fat like stall-fed calves" (Mal 4:2). Their new nature that is united with God is far more honorable and glorified than Adam's first nature because our Lord Jesus Christ

> "abolished in His flesh the enmity, that is, the law of commandments contained in ordinances, so as to create in Himself one new man from the two" (Eph 2:15).
>
> "Therefore, if anyone is in Christ, he is a new creation; old things have passed away; behold, all things have become new" (2 Cor 5:17).

6. Evil power, as far as we are concerned, is real as it dwells in people's hearts, working in our minds, offering us all sorts of evil, negative thoughts and unclean images, stopping us from praying as we should, and enticing us to have worldly desires, going deep into our existence to enslave us. Though Satan is in the air around us and God is also there (as He is everywhere) God is not harmed by being alongside Satan. Likewise, sin and grace can dwell together in the same heart without any change in the nature of the grace of God. As a good servant who shadows his master, following him everywhere and doing nothing without his permission, we should share all our thoughts and intentions with the Lord. He has examined our hearts and known all our needs and already prepared the remedy we need to be healed. Therefore, we ought to turn all our thoughts to Him; putting all our hopes in Him; calling on Him saying:

> "You are my glory, my richness and my father. But You, O Lord, are a shield for me, my glory and the One who lifts up my head. I cried to the Lord with my voice, and He heard me from His holy hill" (Ps 3:3-4).

If you have not yet felt the kind hand of God that will always guide you and His Holy Spirit fully dwelling in your heart to comfort you naturally, at least you should keep the fear of God always in front of you to be very careful not to ever do what hurts His love for you.

Prayer: My Lord, there is a lot of darkness in me that needs You, the Sun of Righteousness, to shine on me to dry out all the evil in me so that I will be united with You and be one with You, as You asked Your Father to do for all of us. Then I will experience Your full power, Your resurrection and Your incomprehensible love.

God who is everywhere rests in our hearts

5. God who has created the whole world out of nothing is unlimited and incomprehensible. Therefore, the heavenly hosts continually say,

> "You are worthy, O Lord, to receive glory and honor and power; For You created all things, and by Your will they exist and were created" (Rev 4:11).

But, gullible people claim that God created the world from a pre-existing material and heretics assert that nature has created itself by its own power. Who is more powerful? Nature, or God who rules over nature? He makes Himself manifest in everything; and is present on earth and in heaven at the same time without moving between the two (not like the angels who descend from heaven to earth). God is in heaven and also here, and also in our hearts; all at the same time. A cynical person could ask how God could be in hell, in darkness or in filthy places. God Himself does not change but contains all things since he is infinite. But Satan, who is his creature, is bound. It is true that God is always superior to everything and all creation. Because of the mystery of the Trinity and His simplicity, the dark forces, although they were created by Him, do not comprehend Him. Nor can evil forces participate in the purity that is in God. Therefore, for God no evil exists as a separate substance, since He is in no way affected by it. John says,

> "In the beginning was the Word, and the Word was with God, and the Word was God. He was in the beginning with God. All things were made through Him, and without Him nothing was made that was made. In Him was life, and the life was the light of men. And the light shines in the darkness, and the darkness did not comprehend it" (Jn 1:1).

God engraves His image on our hearts and souls
7. Like a bee that secretly fashions its honeycomb in the hive, so the Holy Spirit secretly establishes His love in our hearts, changing our bitterness to His sweetness and our roughness into His gentleness. He is like a distinguished artist sculpting a statue, who partly covers some of the features that he is sculpting, until he has finished all his work, and only then he holds it up to shine in the light in front of many people. So the Lord, who is the true artisan, engraves His image on our hearts and secretly renews our souls until our souls leave our bodies. Then He reveals the real beauty of those souls that He has worked on in front of all His saints and angels. This is God's plan for which the Holy Spirit continuously works in us to "be conformed to the image of His Son" (Rom 8:29) and to change our fate back to that which God always hoped for us. As "we have borne the image of the man of dust, we shall also bear the image of the heavenly Man" (1 Cor 15:49). The blessed Saint Paul explained this process of change as he wrote,

> "The body is sown in corruption, it is raised in incorruption. It is sown in dishonor, it is raised in

glory. It is sown in weakness, it is raised in power. It is sown a natural body, it is raised a spiritual body. There is a natural body, and there is a spiritual body. And so, it is written; "The first man Adam became a living being." The last Adam became a life-giving spirit. However, the spiritual is not first, but the natural, and afterward the spiritual" (1 Cor 15:42-46).

"As was the man of dust, so also are those who are made of dust; and as is the heavenly Man, so also are those who are heavenly. And as we have borne the image of the man of dust, we shall also bear the image of the heavenly Man" (1 Cor 15:48-49).

As we are His own workmanship (Eph 2:10), God works in us till we are made vessels of honor in Him, that are full of all good thoughts, which are like precious stones and true pearls. But evil thoughts are contained in vessels that are full of every uncleanness, filthy desires and dead bones.

True Christians are not of this world
8. Christians are not of this world; they are children of the heavenly Adam, a new race, children of the Holy Spirit, shining brothers of Christ, similar to their Father, the spiritual Adam. Therefore, they belong to His city, His race and have His power. The Lord Himself says "you are not of this world, even as I am not of this world" (Jn 17:16). The true Christian is like a merchant who is heading home after successfully completing a long and tedious business journey, who sends word to his friends to prepare a house for him, and to buy him necessary food and furniture. Then when the merchant returns home, his friends and relatives receive him with great

happiness as he brings with him great riches. So also is it with spiritual things. If anyone invests in heavenly riches during their journey on earth, their fellow citizens in heaven (who are the spirits of the saints and the angels) are filled with admiration and say "our brothers who live on earth, have acquired immense riches." Therefore, those who have the Lord with them, on leaving this life, come to meet those living above forever with great happiness. Those who belong to the Lord receive them in heaven as victorious kings and queens; "the nations of those who are saved shall walk in its light, and the kings of the earth bring their glory and honor into it" (Rev 21:24). Our Lord will show us all the good things that He prepared for us when we see Him in heaven. For what is written is true: "I would see the goodness of the Lord in the land of the living" (Ps 27:13). The Lord will clothe each one of us in a white robe and place a crown on each head as He promised:

> "I looked, and behold, a great multitude which no one could number, of all nations, tribes, peoples, and tongues, standing before the throne and before the Lamb, clothed with white robes, with palm branches in their hands" (Rev 7:9).

Prayer: See how wonderful our God is; He secretly works in our souls, hearts and minds to change us into His image so that we all will be vessels of honor, worthy to be revealed in front of all His saints and angels as His magnificent work. Let us leave ourselves fully in His kind hands and wait in hope for His work to be completed in us. In our journey to heaven, let us work on accumulating heavenly riches, which we can take up with us when God will clothe us in white robes washed in His blood as we enter heaven like kings and queens.

Prudent and balanced in every way

9,10. We need prudence and balance in all our ways otherwise we could lose even the good virtues that we think we have obtained. Those who are kind by nature, unless they remain on guard, could find themselves in many troubles. Likewise, those who are wise could be deceived by their own wisdom if they become wise in their own eyes. Therefore, Godly people should be well balanced in all their ways. They should combine mercy with assertiveness, freedom with self-discretion, and words with action. In all their ways, they should put their trust in God and not in themselves. Like good food that needs to be well seasoned with the right spices (not only honey but peppers too), so is virtue that needs to be balanced. Those who claim that there is no sin in man are like people immersed in deep water but still unable to recognize it. They are plunged so deeply into the waves of evil that they deny that there is sin in their minds or thoughts. Some people talk a great deal, but they are not seasoned with heavenly salt. They speak a great deal about the royal table, which they have never eaten from or enjoyed. But only after a person has seen the King, who possesses all the treasures of heaven, then he or she can enter in to inherit all those good things, also inviting other people to come and enjoy God's glory.

11. Like the sorrows of a mother grieving for her only son, so the mind also ought to mourn and shed tears when the soul is dead to God. On the other hand, someone who is covered by God's grace is no longer sad, but is overwhelmed with real joy like someone who has found a great treasure. But, this person may tremble in case he or she loses it, as thieves are always attacking us. A person who has suffered many muggings by robbers and escaped with great difficulty from many dangers, fears loss no more when he later comes to develop great

wealth because of the abundance of his wealth. In the same way, spiritual people who have initially passed through many temptations and then were filled with the grace of the Holy Spirit, are no longer afraid of those who seek to rob them since their wealth is so great. Yet they fear, not with the beginner's fear of evil spirits, but fearing enough to care how they employ the spiritual gifts that have been entrusted to them.

He loves the righteous and has mercy on all the sinners whose chief I am

12. Truly spiritual people each regard themselves as the chief of all sinners. They continuously and genuinely carry this thought with them until it becomes part of their very nature. The more they progress in their knowledge of God, the more they consider themselves to be the most ignorant and unprofitable servants. As the Lord said "when you have done all those things which you are commanded, say 'we are unprofitable servants. We have done what was our duty to do'" (Lk 17:10). The more they study and learn, the less they feel they know while the Holy Spirit acts as their guide. Just as an infant is carried about by his parents who carry him and do with him whatever they wish, so also the Holy Spirit operates in the depths of our souls as the Lord said,

> "the wind blows where it wishes, and you hear the sound of it, but cannot tell where it comes from and where it goes. So is everyone who is born of the Spirit" (Jn 3:8).

The Grace of God feeds the mind and lifts it up to heaven, to the perfect world and to everlasting rest. But in such grace, there are many degrees and perfections. Take the example of those who are given a high-profile job and entrusted with the royal treasury. They are never without fear in case they offend the king in any way. So also, those to whom a spiritual work has been entrusted are always filled with apprehension. And even though they may enjoy some rest, they should live as if they do not really have it. For the kingdom of darkness always wages wars against the souls who love God,

> "for we do not wrestle against flesh and blood, but against principalities, against powers, against the rulers of the darkness of this age, against spiritual hosts of wickedness in the heavenly places" (Eph 6:12).

His treasure is offered to you fully

13. When the grace of the Holy Spirit is delayed for a while, brave people continue to cry out to God in a way that demonstrates the strength of their will and the honesty of their desire for God. Then the Sun of Righteousness, Jesus, shines gloriously in their hearts and His rays penetrate all their members and the greatest peace reigns in power in them. For Christ, their King, sends His heavenly army to capture the devils, chain them and cast them away. "The Sun of Righteousness shall arise with healing in His wings; and you shall go out and grow fat like stall-fed calves" (Mal 4:2).

God has called you to adoption and immortality as He said, "let Us make man in Our image, according to Our likeness" (Gen 1:26). Heaven and earth will pass away, but you have been called to immortality, to be a son, a brother and a spouse of the King. In the things around us, everything that belongs to the bridegroom belongs to the bride as well. So also, everything that belongs to the Lord, no matter how much it is, is entrusted to you.

> "He who overcomes shall inherit all things, and I will be his God and he shall be My son" (Revelation 21:7). This is what Jesus asked His

Father for when He prayed; "the glory which You gave Me I have given them, that they may be one just as We are one: I in them, and You in Me; that they may be made perfect in one" (Jn 17:22-23).

Jesus came to call you in person so that you would receive the treasures that used to be yours.

"I will greatly rejoice in the Lord, My soul shall be joyful in my God; for He has clothed me with the garments of salvation, He has covered me with the robe of righteousness, as a bridegroom decks himself with ornaments, and as a bride adorns herself with her jewels" (Is 61:10).

You should now understand how precious you are in God's eyes and comprehend your dignity with which God has crowned you. The Psalmist, full of the Holy Spirit, rightly deplores those who are not aware of their dignity when he says, "a man who is in honor, yet does not understand, is like the beasts that perish" (Ps 49:20).

Prayer: My Lord, I am the chief of all sinners and the most ignorant among Your children. But You certainly can season me with Your words and give me the reasoned balance that keeps me on the path to heaven with the necessary fear and hope. I cannot comprehend Your love for me; You want me to share Your glory in heaven. Guide me and teach me how to be a true child of Yours.

Glory to the Father and to the Son and to the Holy Spirit forever. Amen.

Chapter 11

The Anointing

Homily 17

We are anointed to be kings
1. The Christians who have been found worthy and who press on for the perfect life in unity with Christ, dedicate themselves always to the cross of Christ as the Lord said: "If anyone desires to come after Me, let him deny himself, and take up his cross, and follow Me" (Mt 16:24). As we can see in the scriptures, the anointing with oil was very awesome (1 Sam 16:13). Likewise, now, those spiritual people who "have an anointing from the Holy One" (1 Jn 2:20) have been anointed with the heavenly oil to be made "kings and priests to His God and Father" (Rev 1:6). As they are captured by the love of Christ, they are taken into a deep experience of God and are crucified with Him and sanctified in Him. In this way, they become children of God and are fully united with Him. Saul, David and others like them who were anointed with natural oil taken from an earthly plant received much honor and became kings. Certainly,

the happiness and honor of those who have been anointed by the Holy Spirit is much greater. Those whose inner man is anointed by the Holy Spirit receive the seal of the kingdom of God, the Holy Spirit Himself, as a guarantee for "He who has prepared us for this very thing is God, who also has given us the Spirit as a guarantee" (2 Cor 5:5). Indeed those who have this seal of the Holy Spirit will be saved from all the punishment that was prepared only for the devil and his followers, as the Holy Spirit Himself revealed to us: "they were commanded not to harm the grass of the earth, or any green thing, or any tree, but only those men who do not have the seal of God on their foreheads" (Revelation 9:4). Immediately, after David was anointed, he had to face many troubles and so do we. But, remember that the Holy Spirit is also called the Comforter because He comforts us in all our tribulations.

2,3. Those whose anointing comes from the true tree of life who is Jesus Christ Himself, are given the privilege of attaining a high spiritual level of life through their adoption by our Lord God. As His children, they partake of the King's secrets and divine gifts through Holy Communion with His true body and precious blood as the Spirit teaches us, "by which have been given to us exceedingly great and precious promises, that through these you may be partakers of the divine nature" (2 Pet 1:4). They freely enter the palace of the Most High with His angels and all the saints during their true spiritual prayers. Though they are still in the world and have not yet received the fulfilment of the promises given to them by our Lord, they enter into the kingdom as if they were already crowned because of the guarantee they have been given. Therefore, while they are still in the body, they understand the abundance of spiritual freedom because they have already tasted the sweetness of God's fatherhood and the effect of His power. It is like the son of a king who has already lived in the royal palace close to his father's throne and so knows all his secrets. At the right time, when he is invited to be crowned, he is not dazed because he is already well trained. Likewise, the Christians who are going to reign with God must become fully immersed in His grace. No one who is untrained, or a stranger to the hidden secrets of God can enter His kingdom and reign with Him. When a person commits sin, the devil puts a veil of darkness over his or her soul. But God's grace comes to completely take it away and return his soul to its original pure state so that he can see the true light of the Sun of Righteousness that will shine into his heart (Mal 4:2).

4. At the end of this world, the righteous people will live in the kingdom of God and see His face as He truly is. For Saint John foretold:

> "when He is revealed, we shall be like Him, for we shall see Him as He is. And everyone who has this hope in Him purifies himself, just as He is pure" (1 Jn 3:2).

However, in this present time, they are captured and taken up to the coming kingdom where they can experience all the beauty of His glory. Though we live on earth passing some of our time dealing with worldly activities, our city is in heaven as Saint Paul affirmed "our citizenship is in Heaven" (Phil 3:20) and "we are fellow citizens with the saints and members of the household of God" (Eph 2:19). Just as the eyes that are open can clearly see the sun, so can the mind that has been fully sanctified see the glory of Christ openly and unite with Him, day and night, in the same way that the Body of Christ unites with the Holy Spirit. People do not reach that spiritual level in a moment but only after many trials, rejection of temptation and much labour in their journey with God that begins now and never ends as they are "being transformed into the same image from glory to glory, just as by the Spirit of the Lord" (2 Cor 3:18). Those people are like the good seeds that fell on good ground, having heard the word with a noble and good heart, then keeping it and bearing fruit with patience (Lk 8:15).

Prayer: My Lord, while I am still on this earth, give me a taste of Your kingdom and confirm my inherence, which You have given me through Your blood. As You transform me into Your image, please help me to labor in love, working out my salvation in reverent fear. I willingly ask You to help me to always be patient in the fiery trials, reject all the influence of evil, focus my mind only on You, so that only Your light and grace is inside me, guiding me in my journey to unity with You.

The reasons for our lack of progress and confusion

5. While we progress in our journey with God, feeling the transformation inside us through the work of the Holy Spirit, occasionally we feel that we have not moved away from our original weakness and our troubled personalities. This always makes us confused regarding the direction and pace of our journey. But we need to understand that God's grace and the enemy's evil power can dwell in the same heart side by side and work against each other to gain influence. As the blessed Paul explained, "the flesh lusts against the Spirit, and the Spirit against the flesh; and these are contrary to one another" (Gal 5:17). Therefore, he advised us that we should "walk in the Spirit, and you shall not fulfil the lust of the flesh" (Gal 5:17) and, "if you are led by the Spirit, you are not under the law" (Gal 5:16). One might wonder how the divine light could be affected by darkness or how the pure heart could be corrupted as it is written, "the light shines in the darkness, and the darkness did

not comprehend it" (Jn 1:5) and, "for what fellowship has righteousness with lawlessness? And what communion has light with darkness?" (2 Cor 6:14). We should not think about these issues only from one aspect. Some people settle in the grace of God and fully rely on it till they become much stronger than sin as they enjoy the life of prayers and peace. However, they always should remain careful because at any time they could fall under the influence of evil thoughts and the trickery of sin. Once inexperienced people feel the work of the grace of God in them, they falsely believe that sin no longer exists in their lives. On the other hand, those who understand well, never dare to deny the trickery of sin and the power of unclean thoughts despite the fact that they live in the grace of God. They know that even when they are living in grace, they are still tested by wicked and unclean thoughts. The apostle clearly warned us to "be vigilant; because your adversary the devil walks about like a roaring lion, seeking whom he may devour" (1 Pet 5:8).

6,7. We have seen many brothers who received great joy and comfort and broke free from all unclean thoughts for a few years, then when they thought that they had completely overcome sin, evil attacked them again from its hiding place. No man with a sound mind believes that when he lives in the grace of God, sin cannot attack him. The fact is that both sin and grace can try, at the same time, to influence the same heart. When grace works in inexperienced people, they think that they have completely conquered the devil and became perfect Christians. But I say that when clouds cover the sun's light and make it dark, the sun, although it is far away, still existing and does not lose anything at all of its nature. Likewise, those who have not yet been completely sanctified still live in God's grace but are held back by sin. Though their natural desires and thoughts are strongly yearning for God, they are not yet fully united with Him in His righteousness as sin still tries to bring them down. Saint Paul talked about this conundrum which those who are not fully united with Christ face:

> "for what I am doing, I do not understand. For what I will to do, that I do not practice; but what I hate, that I do. If then, I do what I will not to do, I agree with the law that it is good. But now, it is no longer I who do it, but sin that dwells in me. For I know that in me (that is, in my flesh) nothing good dwells; for to will is present with me, but how to perform what is good I do not find. For the good that I will to do, I do not do; but the evil I will not to do, that I practice. Now, if I do what I will not to do, it is no longer I who do it, but sin that dwells in me" (Rom 7:15-19).

On the other hand, there are people who are held deeply by grace though they still experience unclean thoughts from the evil one. Therefore, the whole issue needs a lot of understanding and good judgment.

8. Some people think that the soul has no weakness after receiving grace, but in fact, God requires a person's free will to allow both the soul and the Holy Spirit to work together in full harmony. Some people who have grace care only about themselves, but others seek to benefit their brothers and sisters. Certainly, the latter are better than the former. While some in their quest for righteousness succeed in hiding themselves in their secret place (Mt 6:6), others tend to seek false glory and vain praise of men. Our goodwill towards God is made complete and truly effective by our free will working in harmony with the Holy Spirit. Therefore,

Saint Paul teaches us not to quench the Spirit (1 Thess 5:19).

9,10,11,12. Those who talk about the spiritual life without personal experience of it are like a poor man who sees himself in a dream as a very rich man but he wakes up only to find out that he is still the same poor man. It seems that all they have is the external appearance and illusions. In the same manner, it is easy to talk about renouncing the world and all its bad desires but the experience of reaching this level is not easy at all. Also, I liken them to a man who can describe that honey is sweet but has never tasted it. But in 1 Corinthians (3:1-4), the apostle traces out how the work of purifying the heart must be done with patience and perseverance; teaching that at first, the believers are fed with milk as babies then after, there can be growth to full perfection. Just as it is impossible for fish to live outside of water, or a human being to walk without feet or to see light without eyes, so also no one can know the mysteries of God or receive the riches which make him a true Christian without our Lord Jesus and His divine power. The Holy Spirit guides those who are truly wise. They are not like Greek philosophers who are only eloquent in speech. True Christians don't rely on the wisdom of speech (2 Cor 11:6), they are genuinely righteous as they fully acknowledge the Kingdom of God "not in word, but in power" (1Cor 4:20).

Christianity is sustenance

13. Christianity is substance, indeed, food and drink! The more you eat from it, the more you love it and your heart longs for it more as you continue eating from it and never feel full. It is like a very thirsty man who is given a reviving drink, he always asks for more. Truly, the taste of the Sprit is just the same but without any

limits. I can never accurately liken it to anything! This is not just mere talk, it is the real work of the Holy Spirit who acts quietly in the heart. Some think they have become saints only because they decided to remain celibate or to attain other visible things, but they are not saints if sin is still in their hearts and minds. The true saint is one who is cleansed and sanctified in the inner man by the Holy Spirit, as Saint Paul taught:

> "For he is not a Jew who is one outwardly, nor is circumcision that which is outward in the flesh; but he is a Jew who is one inwardly; and circumcision is that of the heart, in the Spirit, not in the letter; whose praise is not from men but from God." (Rom 2:28-29).

14, 15. When the Jews were in charge of the priesthood, some were persecuted because of their perseverance in the truth such as Eleazar and the Maccabees. Also, now, after the cross and the tearing of the veil in the temple, some Christians are persecuted similarly. Troubles come to the true Christians to give them a chance to witness to the truth, but they must continue to be watchful so they don't fall. One of the brothers had a vision of the heavenly Jerusalem while he was praying, but sadly, after a short while he fell into sin as he became proud. If that man who saw the heavenly Jerusalem fell, how can an ordinary man say because I fast, pray and have distributed money to the poor, I have become holy? "For many walk, of whom I have told you often, and now tell you even weeping, that they are the enemies of the cross of Christ" (Phil 3:18-19). Perfection is not only giving up evil acts. It can only happen when the Holy Spirit enters your ragged heart and kills the old evil serpent (Gen 3:1), that is still hiding in the secret place of your mind which is the subconscious. When the old serpent is destroyed and dragged out, the whole of you will become pure and clean. All the law and the prophets, and especially the coming of our Lord Jesus Christ, aim to make us clean and pure. Therefore, we must persevere in our quest to achieve this purity in our hearts.

Certainly, there is no other way forward but through Him who was crucified for us, for Jesus said: "I am the vine, you are the branches. He who abides in Me, and I in him, bears much fruit; for without Me you can do nothing" (Jn 15:5). Jesus is the way, the truth and the life (Jn 14:6), the door (Jn 10:9), the pearl (Mt 13:45-46), and the heavenly living bread (Jn 6:51). Without Him it is impossible for us to know the truth or be saved. Therefore remember that all the material things of this world benefit you nothing, as Saint Paul declares:

> "Yet indeed I also count all things loss for the excellence of the knowledge of Christ Jesus my Lord, for whom I have suffered the loss of all things, and count them as rubbish, that I may gain Christ" (Phil 3:8).

You must give up any knowledge, eloquence of speech or ability to debate that you might have acquired over the years and consider it all rubbish in order to be built up by the foolishness of the word of preaching. Live by these words: "for the message of the cross is foolishness to those who are perishing, but to us who are being saved it is the power of God" (1 Cor 1:18) and "for since in the wisdom of God the world by its wisdom did not know God, God was pleased to save those who believe by the foolishness of preaching" (1 Cor 1:21) as "the foolishness of God is wiser than human wisdom, and the weakness of God is stronger than human strength" (1 Cor 1:25). Therefore, our preaching should not rely on fancy speech or worldly glory but on the true wisdom from God, which is very effective through the power of the cross.

Prayer: My Lord, now I know that life with You is not a set of external appearances, empty words or practices but it is reality and the more I live in it, the more I love it. It is indeed as real as eating and drinking. Please help me to discover Your plan for me. Prepare me to give up everything that ever gave me fake security or false satisfaction. Please come to my heart to carry me over into a new life and to kill all evil that was brought into my heart by Satan, the old serpent.

Glory to the Holy Trinity who is of one consubstantial essence. Amen.

Chapter 12

True Richness

Homily 18

The treasure of the Holy Spirit
    1,2. In your life, you must have met people who are genuinely very rich and others who try hard to appear as if they are rich. You can certainly tell the difference between the two. People who are extremely wealthy can simply buy whatever they wish and accumulate all the valuable things they ever wanted relying on their earthly treasures without second thoughts. The same are those who diligently seek God and find His heavenly treasure – the treasure of the Holy Spirit. They easily complete all the virtues of righteousness with enjoyment and love relying only on the abundance of the spiritual gifts, which they receive through Him. But those who are poor go through many troubles trying to attain even some richness through a lot

of suffering and struggling. Those who have the treasure of the Holy Spirit maintain the purity of their bodies and hearts with the simplicity of their eyes and thoughts, without any feeling of being deprived from any leisure of this world, nor any sense of struggle, as they are united with Him in all they do. Through this treasure they can easily fulfil all the fullness of righteousness and do all the commandments of the Lord without hardship. They keep simple eyes, pure hearts, clean bodies and heavenly thoughts without much struggle as they have it all in that treasure given to them in the Holy Spirit, who continuously takes from Jesus and gives them according to their need in due time, as Jesus revealed: "He will glorify Me, for He will take of what is Mine and declare it to you (Jn 16:14). When you have this treasure even when you are still weak and unworthy, you actually join in with a lot of holy people led by Saint Paul exclaiming, "we have this treasure in earthen vessels, that the excellence of the power may be of God and not of us (2 Cor 4:7). All rich people try to keep their treasures in safe places as they realize the never-ending risk that thieves could break in and take it all away. But, our God has given the treasure of the Holy Spirit to those who honestly desire to possess Him securely inside themselves in this life as He said; "whoever desires, let him take the water of life freely (Rev 22:17). God Himself becomes our righteousness and richness, also as Saint Paul also said: "but of Him you are in Christ Jesus, who became for us wisdom from God—and righteousness and sanctification and redemption" (1Cor 1:30). Therefore, those who have found and possessed in themselves the heavenly treasure of the Spirit easily fulfil all the commandments justly and complete all the virtues in purity and without blame. They do so with great ease and with no need to force themselves to do it. They find that following God's commandments is not only easy but also enjoyable as our Lord declared, "My yoke is easy and My burden is light" (Mt 11:29-30).

3. Therefore, every person should compel himself or herself to beg the Lord to make him or her worthy to find and receive the heavenly treasure of the Holy Spirit in order to be able to follow all the Lord's commandments in ease and perfection with purity and without fault, even those commandments which he or she failed to do before despite trying as hard as he or she could. For the soul that has found the Lord, the real treasure, through the action of the Spirit, in strong faith, unfailing hope and continuous patience, enjoys the fruit of the Spirit in ease and peace. It is God's pleasure to fill us with the Holy Spirit when we ask Him sincerely, as He spoke to us: "If you then, being evil, know how to give good gifts to your children, how much more will your heavenly Father give the Holy Spirit to those who ask Him!" (Lk 11:13).

The riches of the Spirit and serving others

4,5. Again, take the example of a wealthy man who wants to throw a party; he spends a lot of money out of his treasure without any worry regarding the cost. Therefore, he shows great generosity to his guests serving them delicacies; plenty of food and drink prepared in the most diligent way. On the other hand, someone who is poor and who wants to make a dinner for his friends has to borrow everything needed such as crockery, utensils, cutlery, tablecloths, and everything else, and then he has to return it all back when the dinner is over. Obviously, after he has returned everything, he no longer possesses any of it, as he did not have his own riches that could have satisfied him. In the same manner, those who are rich in fellowship with Holy Spirit and have true heavenly assets, speak of the treasure they possess inside them when they speak to others about the word of truth. Out of their treasure they edify and give joy to those who listen to them, as our Lord conveyed that "every scribe instructed concerning the kingdom of heaven is like a householder who brings out of his treasure things new and old" (Mt 13:52). They never fear that their wealth will dwindle, as the treasure of heavenly righteousness dwells in them, from which they draw to give others. But those who are poor have neither the riches of Christ in them nor spiritual wealth. Spiritual wealth is the spring of all righteous gifts whether talking, doing, thinking or revealing godly secrets which nobody can utter. Even when one of those poor people speaks the word of truth to enlighten others—without having in him the word of God in power and truth—he only manages to repeat from his memory what has been borrowed from parts of the gospel or heard in previous sermons given by spiritual people. In this manner, he is only imagining himself to be enriching others, who might seem to be enjoying his talk. But when he has finished, he has to give back everything he has pontificated about and goes back to being poor again because he has never owned the treasure of the Spirit from which he could have drawn to help and refresh others, and he himself is not refreshed nor does he rejoice in the spirit.

6. For this reason, we ought to ask God in perseverance and faith to show us His riches in our hearts, which are the true treasure of Christ in the power of the Holy Spirit. When we first find the Lord inside ourselves (who benefits us with salvation and eternal life) then we can benefit others. In this way, we will be taking from Christ (the treasure of righteousness dwelling inside us) to give to those who need the words of virtue which disclose all the heavenly secrets. For this is the pleasure of the Father to dwell in everyone who

loves Him and believes in Him. Our Lord expressed that "He who loves Me will be loved by My Father, and I will love him and manifest Myself to him" (Jn 14:21). And He also said; "If anyone loves Me, he will keep My word; and My Father will love him, and We will come to him and make Our home with him" (Jn 14:23). This is the desire of the Father, the pleasure of Christ and the promise of the Holy Spirit. Glory to the inconceivable kindness of the Holy Trinity.

Different experiences during our quest for the treasure of the Holy Sprit

7,8,9. If you wonder about the many different stages that you might experience while seeking the Holy Spirit, you need to know that those who have been given "the right to become children of God" (Jn 1:12), and to be born again of the Holy Spirit are led by Him through many different paths while the grace of God continues to work secretly in their hearts to give them spiritual joy. Sometimes, the grace of God gives them joy and cheerfulness, similar to a royal banquet where they are filled with the utmost happiness and contentment. At other times, they are like a joyful bride in a great, loving partnership with the bridegroom, resting in heavenly peace. They are like angels with no earthly bodies as their bodies become light as they have lightened themselves from fleshly desires. On other occasions, they cry and lament over the entire human race as they pray for all human beings, burning with love inside them towards everyone. Or the Spirit rekindles the fire of joy and love inside them which makes them desire, if possible, to take everyone into their hearts not discriminating between good and bad people. But sometimes, in the humility of the Spirit, they feel they are below all other people and consider themselves lesser than them and the least of human beings. In other times, the soul finds itself in great peace, tranquillity and gentleness with no feelings other than the utmost inexplicable spiritual pleasure, rest and well-being.

At other moments, the grace of God teaches the soul many things that cannot be explained in words or speech. But, in other times the soul remains like one of the ordinary people. Therefore, we can conclude that the grace of God deals with the spiritual person in many different ways. The Spirit leads the soul, which grace refreshes and revives in many different ways according to God's good will, and trains it in a variety of ways to bring it back to the heavenly Father, pure and perfect and with no fault.

Prayer: My Lord, let me find You inside me so I can fully enjoy the treasure of the Holy Spirit who will help me to obey You and guide me on my way to You. Work with me so that I can be perfect as You are, all light, all love and all righteousness. Give me the grace of Your Holy Spirit to train me till I find my way safely to Your kingdom.

How can we who have been saved do evil again?!

10. These various pleasures of grace, though many, work without ceasing in people who are not far from perfection. When the soul reaches that level of spiritual perfection, it becomes completely purified from all lust and joins with the Holy Spirit in an indescribable partnership. Finally, when it becomes worthy to join with the Holy Spirit, then it becomes all light, all eyes *(see Homily 1)*, all spirit, all joy, all rest, all happiness, all love, all compassion, all righteousness and all goodness. As a stone at the bottom of the sea is immersed in sea water, so people like these who are totally immersed in the Holy Spirit become like Christ; putting on the virtues of the power of the Spirit with no further change as they

become pure and faultless from the inside out. Saint Paul explained that we should "put on the Lord Jesus Christ, and make no provision for the flesh, to fulfil its lusts" (Rom 13:14).

11. Having been restored by the Spirit and returned back to God, how can they bring forth any fruit of sin? But the fruit of the Spirit shines forth in them all the time and under all circumstances. Therefore, let us implore God in faith, love and abundant hope to give us this heavenly grace, the grace of the Holy Spirit, to rule over us and govern our behavior and thoughts and to lead us according to God's will. In this way, through the work of the Spirit in us, we will become worthy to attain the perfect fullness of Christ (Eph 3:19). He also gives us all grace to become one with the "perfect man, to the measure of the stature of the fullness of Christ" (Eph 4:13). The Lord has promised all this to those who believe in Him and ask in truth to be given the unspeakable mysteries of communion with the Holy Spirit. Therefore, let us consecrate of our souls entirely to our Lord Jesus Christ. Let us hurry to receive all these good things that the Lord has prepared for us. As we consecrate our souls and bodies, nailing them to the cross of our Lord Christ, let us also be worthy and ready for His kingdom glorifying the Father, the Son and the Holy Spirit. Amen.

Chapter 13

Be Filled with the Holy Spirit

Homily 19

How can I be filled with the Holy Spirit?
1. If you desire to come to the Lord and to be deemed worthy of His eternal life, to be a dwelling place for Christ, and to be filled with the Holy Spirit so that you may produce the fruits of the Spirit, you ought to do the following: begin with an unshakeable faith as Saint Paul taught us "above all, taking the shield of faith" (Eph 6:16); give yourself wholly to the words of His commandments for

> "the word of God is living and powerful, and sharper than any two-edged sword, piercing even to the division of soul and spirit, and of joints and marrow, and is a discerner of the thoughts and intents of the heart" (Heb 4:12);

clear your mind from all earthly concerns by renouncing the world altogether; "do not love the world or the things in the world." (1 Jn 2:15); persevere always in prayers, "continue earnestly in prayer, being vigilant in it with thanksgiving" (Col 4:2), asking the Lord in faith and trust, to come to dwell in you, to shape you into a perfect person and strengthen you so that you can keep all His commandments; "that Christ may dwell in your hearts through faith; that you, being rooted and grounded in love" will understand the love of Christ (Eph 3:17); wait in faith for the Lord's manifestation to you, in spite of circumstances and timing till He comes to you in His ultimate love; "I will look to the Lord; I will wait for the God of my salvation; my God will hear me" (Mic 7:7); To direct your mind towards Him as He said, "Son of man, look with your eyes and hear with your ears, and fix your mind on everything I show you" (Ezk 40:4), and consider that; "Him we preach, warning every man and teaching every man in all wisdom, that we may present every man perfect in Christ Jesus" (Colossians 1:28); then, force yourself to do every good work and to fulfil all the Lord's commandments till it becomes second nature to you. Similarly, you should train yourself to be merciful, kind, compassionate and righteous to the utmost of your power as the Lord said, "be merciful, just as your Father also is merciful" (Lk 6:36). Also, you should force yourself to have a humble mind and to consider yourself less than all other people. As our Lord recounted: "from the days of John the Baptist until now the kingdom of heaven suffers violence, and the violent take it by force" (Mt 11:12); do not seek any honor, praise, or glory from anyone as it is written, "how can you believe, who receive honour from one another, and do not seek the honour that comes from the only God?" (Jn 5:44); always put the Lord and His commandments in front of your eyes, wishing for nothing other than to please the Lord in meekness of heart as the Lord said, "learn from Me, for I am gentle and lowly in heart, and you will find rest for your souls" (Mt 11:29) and He also said, "if you love Me, keep My commandments" (Jn 14:15).

> "You shall bind them as a sign on your hand, and they shall be as frontlets between your eyes. You shall write them on the doorposts of your house and on your gates" (Deut 6:8-9).

When the Lord dwells in you
2. When the Lord dwells in you, all that you used to force yourself to do reluctantly, you will do willingly and easily in love. When you become mindful of the Lord, waiting for Him with an abundance of love in the Holy Spirit, the Lord will see your constant desire and diligence and how you have tamed your heart to do all good things even against your own nature. Then He will show you compassion and free you from the deep-seated and hidden sins which previously overpowered you. He will fill you with the Holy Spirit; "blessed are those who hunger and thirst for righteousness, for they shall be filled" (Mt 5:6). Thus, afterwards, you will find it very easy to do all the commandments of the Lord without any difficulty and without forcing yourself because it will be the Lord Himself, dwelling in you, who fulfils His own commandments in you. Following this, you will produce the fruits of the Spirit in all purity. It is clear now that "it is God who works in you both to will and to do for His good pleasure" (Phil 2:13).

Start by forcing yourself to receive the support from the Most High
3,4. People who want to come to the Lord must force themselves to do what is good even if it is against the natural desire of their hearts, always waiting for the mercy of the Lord in unshakeable faith. You should force

yourself to love when you are short of love, to be meek when you are short of meekness, to pray when you have no spiritual prayers, and to do kind deeds when you have no charity in your heart. Also, you need to force yourself to bear humiliation patiently when you are looked down on and you should not be angry when you are made light of or put to shame as it is written, "do not avenge yourselves" (Rom 12:19). Thus, when the Lord sees you striving and compelling yourself in spite of the resistance of your own heart, then He gives you true spiritual prayers and true love, in addition to meekness, kindness and true charity. In summary, He fills you up with the fruit of His Holy Spirit for "those who, having heard the word with a noble and good heart, keep it and bear fruit with patience" (Lk 8:15). But, those who do not have faith and do not trust that the Lord will complete all His works in them, do not receive much from the Lord. They need to try harder with unshakeable faith, asking the Lord to give them all their spiritual needs as He remind us, "ask, and it will be given to you; seek, and you will find; knock, and it will be opened to you (Lk 11:9).

Prayer: How wonderful our God is; He looks at our honest desire to fulfil His commandments and gives us all we need to be united with Him. Every time we force ourselves to do His will, we demonstrate our love for Him. He will certainly make our struggle easy and sweet, so we can attain all the virtues and get rid of all the darkness inside us by asking Him faithfully to do this in our prayers. Then He will do the rest for us.

6,7. When the Lord observes your earnestness to compel your heart to do all goodness, and to be filled with simplicity, charity, meekness, love and prayers, He gives you His whole self; the Lord himself in truth does all these things in you purely, without labour or coercion. As a result, you can then practice naturally all those things which you could not force yourself to do previously, because of the sin that dwelt in you. For when God abides in you and you in Him, the Lord Himself performs all His own commandments in you without effort, filling you with the fruit of the Spirit. As you become a partaker of the Holy Spirit, God makes the gift of the Holy Spirit in you grow and thrive, as the Holy Spirit rests in your humility, charity and meekness. Remember that God said, "he who eats My flesh, and drinks My blood, abides in Me, and I in him" (Jn 6:56). We should all prepare ourselves in this manner to do all goodness with all our ability. If the grace of God came to those who asked for it while they were still not prepared for it, they could easily lose it or even fall because of pride, or at least they would not grow in it since they had not given themselves completely to the commandments of the Lord by their full free will. For the place where the Holy Spirit dwells is a humble, meek and charitable heart, as the Lord commanded.

Think little of yourself and trust in God

5. For as every one of us forces and compels himself or herself to pray despite the reluctance of his or her own heart, we should also force ourselves to trust God. You also ought to think little of yourself and to consider yourself the least of all people; and so not engage in foolish conversations but rather always contemplate the word of God and talk about Him. Also, you should not be angry or boisterous as it is written, "let all bitterness, wrath, anger, clamour, and evil speaking be put away from you, with all malice" (Eph 4:31). Moreover, you need to walk in all God's ways in righteousness, meekness and humility; so that you are not proud or puffed up or speak evil against anyone as you know that "He has scattered the proud in the

imagination of their hearts (Lk 1:51). The humble person never falls. Therefore, let us force our hearts to be humble even if our hearts may dislike it, and let us coerce ourselves further to be meek and charitable, praying consistently to God in faith, hope and love to send His Holy Spirit to fill our hearts that we may pray and worship Him "in spirit and truth" (Jn 4:24).

Prayer: My Lord, abide in me that You may do your will in me and fill me with all the grace of Your Holy Spirit. Give me Your meekness that I may become a dwelling place for You. Prepare me for Your kingdom as an heir and a child of Yours.

Humility and the grace of God are cofactors

8. When the Spirit bestows all these things on you, He teaches you true prayers, true love and true meekness which you may previously have sought by forcing yourself into it. But now it will all be given freely to you. Jesus said that the Holy Spirit "will take of what is Mine and declare it to you" (Jn 16:14) and, "I am the vine, you are the branches. He who abides in Me, and I in him, bears much fruit; for without Me you can do nothing" (Jn 15:5). When you have grown in God and been perfected by Him, you will be counted as an heir of the heavenly kingdom as "justified by his grace, we should become heirs according to the hope of eternal life" (Titus 3:7).

The unutterable longing of the Holy Spirit for us

9. May the Holy Spirit pray in us, for the Spirit himself teaches us true prayer and give us true humility that we previously failed to attain.

> "The Spirit also helps in our weaknesses. For we do not know what we should pray for as we ought, but the Spirit Himself makes intercession for us

with groanings which cannot be uttered" (Rom 8:26).

In the same manner, God who said; "My yoke is easy and My burden is light" (Mt 11:30), makes us truly fruitful by filling us with all the fruit of the Spirit. In this way, the Spirit Himself, who knows the will of God, fulfils all the commandments of the Lord in us, without pain or coercion, till He perfects us as we are in Him and grows in us, cleansing us from every sin, bringing our souls to Christ as beautiful brides "not having spot or wrinkle or any such thing" (Eph 5:27) as we rest in Christ's kingdom and He rests in us for evermore.

Glory to His kindness, His mercies and His love, for He gave all this glory to human beings. He gave them the right to become children of the Heavenly Father and called them to become His brothers. Glory to Him forever more.

Chapter 14

Put On the Spirit and Let It Adorn You

Homily 20

If you are not covered with the Holy Spirit, you are naked

1,2. Saint Paul taught us "if anyone does not have the Spirit of Christ, he is not His" (Rom 8:9). If you are not clothed with the Holy Spirit, then you are naked. Therefore, cry out to the Lord asking Him to clothe you with His heavenly robe which is His Holy Spirit, for He gives the Holy Spirit to those who ask Him, as He promised, "if you then, being evil, know how to give good gifts to your children, how much more will your heavenly Father give the Holy Spirit to those who ask Him!" (Lk 11:13). As nakedness is a terrible disgrace that produces a feeling of shame, the person who is not covered by the Holy Spirit is only covered by the shame of wrong desires. When the first man, Adam, found himself naked he felt ashamed, vulnerable, weak and afraid. Many see nakedness as a terrible shame; friends and family turn away if they see a loved one naked. Even Noah's children could not look at him when he was found naked (Gen 9:20-24). In the same manner, God's face turns away from the souls that are not clothed with the Holy Spirit, in the full assurance of faith (Heb 10: 22) because they did not put on the Lord Jesus Christ in power and truth. But for us, as we "put on the Lord Jesus Christ, and make no provision for the flesh, to fulfil its lusts" (Rom 13:14), we unite with Him in order to not be found naked. If bodily nakedness brings so much shame, how much greater is the shame of the soul that is not clothed with the heavenly spiritual robe! Everyone who is not covered by this divine glory ought to feel ashamed and to declare it to the Lord, as Adam felt ashamed of his nakedness when he declared "I heard Your voice in the garden, and I was afraid because I was naked; and I hid myself" (Gen 3:10).

Though Adam made himself a cover from fig leaves, he continued to feel ashamed as he recognised his disgrace, poverty and nakedness. For fig leaves were not enough to give him reassurance or confidence. Therefore, you ought not to make yourself a false cover from self-righteousness or vain glory but to ask Christ to cover you with the genuine garment of the true light of His indescribable glory for He is "the true Light which gives light to every man coming into the world" (Jn 1:9).

Christ is our righteousness

3. Christ is our righteousness for He is our sanctification and redemption, "you are in Christ Jesus, who became for us wisdom from God—and righteousness and sanctification and redemption" (1 Cor 1:30). If you rely on your own righteousness, your labour ends up in vain without any fruit, for our righteousness

is like filthy rags as Isaiah said "But we are all like an unclean thing, and all our righteousness are like filthy rags; we all fade as a leaf, and our iniquities, like the wind, have taken us away" (Is 64:6). Let us ask God then to clothe us with the robe of salvation that is the Lord Jesus Himself who is the indescribable light. We must never take Him off again but unite with Him till our bodies are glorified in the light of His resurrection according to Saint Paul who taught us that "He who raised Christ from the dead will also give life to your mortal bodies through His Spirit who dwells in you" (Rom 8:11).

> Therefore, He said; "I counsel you to buy from Me gold refined in the fire, that you may be rich; and white garments, that you may be clothed, that the shame of your nakedness may not be revealed; and anoint your eyes with eye salve, that you may see" (Rev 3:18).

Prayer: My Lord, I beg you to cover me with Your Holy Spirit that I will not be found naked when I stand in front of You. I have tried all the false covers including self-pride, impressive knowledge, belonging to a group of influential leaders or financial abundance but all of it left me still naked, insecure and unsatisfied. Please, clothe me with the robe of righteousness that is You. Therefore, help me to guard the robe You have given me as You said; "Behold, I am coming as a thief. Blessed is he who watches, and keeps his garments, lest he walk naked and they see his shame" (Rev 16:15).

Christ is our physician
4,5. Our old enemy, Satan, managed in his treachery to deeply wound Adam and darken his mind to make him desire lust and accept sin in order to blind him from seeing the heavenly treasures of God. The woman

who had a flow of blood (Mk 5:25-29) was immediately healed when she truly believed and touched Him. In the same manner, every soul that has been wounded by sin and flooded by unclean thoughts will be completely healed from all that incurable weakness and guilt if only it comes to Christ in true faith. Only Jesus can stop that fountain of unclean thoughts and heal that deeply infected wound. Adam was indeed so badly wounded that only the Lord himself could heal him because He is the Lamb who came to take away the sins of the whole world (Jn 1:29). The woman with a flow of blood spent all her possessions to be cured by those who claimed to be able to cure her but failed until she came to the Lord in faith, touching the hem of His garment and at once feeling the sign of healing in her body. In the same manner, a soul that has been deeply wounded by evil passion, can be cured by no one but the Lord Himself.

6. Moses came offering priesthood, gifts, sacrifices, Sabbaths, tithes, new moons, burnt offerings and many other means of righteousness but never succeeded in giving an effective cure to the soul. This was all a shadow of the real things to come. All the righteousness that came through the law failed to heal humanity, till the saviour, the true physician, who cures without cost came to give His life as a ransom for the healing of all mankind. He set us free from bondage, brought us out of darkness and glorified us in His own light. Therefore, it was fitting and proper that Jesus said; "He has sent Me to heal the broken hearted, to proclaim liberty to the captives and recovery of sight to the blind, to set at liberty those who are oppressed" (Lk 4:18). Let us give all of our hearts and minds to the Lord who will surely come and heal us completely from all the sins that tricked us and wounded us deep in our souls, then we will find our rest in Him and comprehend all of His love.

Ask and you will certainly be given

7. Only the medicine of the Holy Spirit could heal the whole earth from that invisible plague. Indeed, only the medicine of the Holy Spirit can cure people, washing them in their hearts, so they can live. The woman who certainly could not find a cure for herself, found the will to come to the Lord. Also, the blind man who could not cross the road on his own, managed to find his voice to cry out; "Jesus son of David have mercy on me" (Mk 10:46 -52). When he believed, he found the cure from the Lord who came to him and made him see again. So every one of us is like this too. Though you are undone by vile affections and blinded by the darkness of sin, when you find the willpower to cry out asking Jesus to come to you, He will certainly come to give you His eternal deliverance.

8. Had not the blind man cried out, and had not the woman with the flow of blood touched the Lord, they would not have found a cure. Unless a person comes to the Lord by his or her own free will, with a pure heart and pure intentions, asking Him for help with the full assurance of faith, he or she will find no cure. The Spirit taught us saying, "from there you will seek the Lord your God, and you will find Him if you seek Him with all your heart and with all your soul" (Deut 4:29). They were cured with immediate effect, but we struggle because of the weakness of our faith. You should know that the Lord, as a good and caring physician, takes far more interest in our immortal souls than our corruptible bodies. When your soul gains clear sight, you will say with David the prophet, "open my eyes, that I may see wondrous things from Your law" (Ps 119:18) and you shall never be blind again. We have not yet found the spiritual cure because of our divided minds, because of our unbelief and

because we do not fully love Him with all our hearts. Let us then truly believe in Him and come to Him in truth and spirit (Jn 4:23), that He may work His true cure in us speedily.

Remember, He promised to give the Holy Spirit to those who ask Him (Lk 11:13) and to open to those who knock (Lk 11:9) and to be found by those who seek Him.

> "Ask and it will be given to you; seek and you will find; knock and the door will be opened for you. For everyone who asks receives, and the one who seeks finds, and to the one who knocks, the door will be opened" (Mt 7:7-8).

We know that; "what He had promised He was also able to perform" (Rom 4:21).

Prayer: My Lord, I am indeed "wretched, miserable, poor, blind, and naked" (Rev 3:17). I can do nothing about it but cry out to You saying; "Son of David, have mercy on me" (Mk 10:47). Heal me, cleanse me and form me in Your image again. Let me put You on, so cover me with the grace of Your Holy Spirit so that I will never be found naked ever again.

Glory to Him forever. Amen

Chapter 15

External and Internal Spiritual Warfare

Homily 21: Christians fight the devil and his trickery as good soldiers as Saint Paul told his disciple Timothy; "my son, be strong in the grace that is in Christ Jesus... You therefore must endure hardship as a good soldier of Jesus Christ" (2 Tim 2: 1-3). In spiritual warfare, the true Christian fights on two fronts: external and internal. The external war concerns issues that we have to deal with in our daily life that are usually caused by earthly desires and worldly distractions. Meanwhile the internal war is in the heart, caused by the counsels of the spirits of wickedness. The one who truly wishes to please God must stand steadfastly against the wicked enemy and fight on those two fronts.

The evil bonds of external and internal wars

1. The external war is centred around the visible matters of this world which act as thorns that hinder us from becoming fruitful, as the Lord taught "the cares of

this world, the deceitfulness of riches, and the desires for other things entering in choke the word, and it becomes unfruitful" (Mk 4:19). Therefore, we need to fully detach ourselves from the care of this world and to withdraw from the love of the earthly desires and lusts. The internal fight happens in the hidden parts, in the heart and mind, against the wicked spirits as Saint Paul said

> "For we do not wrestle against flesh and blood, but against principalities, against powers, against the rulers of the darkness of this age, against spiritual hosts of wickedness in the heavenly places" (Eph 6:12).

2. When mankind transgressed the commandment of God and consequently was exiled from paradise, he was bound in two different ways by two different bonds. The first bond is related to this life; the care for this life, the love of the world which is manifested in mortal pleasures and sinful desires; the love of wealth, worldly glory, public honour, possessions, relationships, special places, expensive clothes and all the other earthly things that feed our bodily senses. The word of God, working in us, encourages us all to make our own wilful decision to loosen ourselves from this earthly bond. This decision has to be made by our own free will because through our own free will we were bound by this earthly bond. When someone is made free of this bond, he or she can keep God's commandments fully.

The second bond is made of the chains of darkness, which are under the influence of the evil spirits that hedge the soul all around. Consequently, those who are bound become unable to love the Lord, as they would like, nor can they believe as they should, nor can they pray as they wish as they find it all difficult because of visible or invisible adversaries. This sort of resistance has been sown and grown since the first man transgressed.

The word of God liberates us
3. The word of God is mighty and capable of freeing us from the deepest bonds of sin and hidden sources of weakness as the Lord said, "if you abide in My word, you are My disciples indeed. And you shall know the truth, and the truth shall make you free" (Jn 8:31-32). When people listen to the word of God and accept it fully and so fight the good fight, casting away the care of this life and loosening themselves from the love of this world, rejecting all fleshly pleasure and praying continuously, then they become able to discover the hidden war inside their hearts. They find out the sources of the hidden internal resistance that had been sown in them by the wicked spirits. Thus, standing steadfastly in prayers, calling on the Lord in faith without doubting and with much patience, expecting heavenly support and protection, they will be enabled to receive from the Lord true freedom from the hidden internal bonds of the evil attacks that work in them forming lust and unholy desires. As the Lord said, "you are already clean because of the word which I have spoken to you" (Jn 15:3), as "He might sanctify and cleanse her with the washing of water by the word" (Eph 5:26).

Prayer: My Lord, free me from those external and internal bonds that weakened my will, darkened my thoughts, distracted me and made me unfruitful. Please, heal me by Your word and cleanse me. I do not wish to spend the rest of my life shackled by those invisible bonds. Only You can set me free and make me will and do (Phil 2:13).

4. These wars can only be brought to a favourable end by the grace and power of God. No people can save

themselves from the errors of thoughts, uncontrolled passions and the trickery of the evil one by themselves or by their own power especially as; "we are all like an unclean thing, and all our righteousness are like filthy rags" (Is 64:6). If someone is entangled by the different affairs of this world; interlocked in various earthly ties; carried away by the evil lusts, he or she will even fail to discover the war raging internally. But, when people wilfully decide to loosen themselves from the visible bonds of this world and its fleshly pleasures, and begin to wait constantly for the Lord; emptying themselves from all worldly desires, they then become alert and aware of the whole internal war of evil desires. To emphasise further; unless people make a genuine effort, deny the world and loosen themselves from all earthly desires, they will fail to understand the trickery of the wicked spirits and so will remain strangers from their true selves as Saint Anthony the Great rightly said, "he who has known himself, has known God."

The armor of the Holy Spirit

5. People who have truly renounced the world and cast away all their earthly burdens and who have put off all bodily lusts and desires for human glory and all false honour and who have decided in their hearts to steadfastly serve and worship the Lord and to fully unite with Him, will discover the unseen bonds of hidden passions and secret wars inside them. As they implore the Lord for help, they receive heavenly support which is the armour of the Holy Spirit that Saint Paul described as

> "having girded your waist with truth, having put on the breastplate of righteousness, and having shod your feet with the preparation of the gospel of peace; above all, taking the shield of faith with which you will be able to quench all the fiery darts

of the wicked one. And take the helmet of salvation, and the sword of the Spirit, which is the word of God" (Eph 6:14-17).

People who have this armor are indeed able to stand steadfastly against all the trickery of the devil even if the wicked spirits surround them.

Chapter 16

Victory in Spiritual Warfare

Homily 23

Whoever is born of the Holy Spirit puts on Christ as a jewel.

1. A royal crown is always decorated with the most precious jewels; fit only for king. Therefore, no one else is allowed to wear anything decorated with such gems, as he who wears it will be taken for a king. Thus, unless one is born of the royal and divine Holy Spirit and becomes part of the royal family of God, he or she cannot wear the heavenly and most precious jewel, which is the image of light that is the Lord Himself. That person becomes a child of God according to what is written: "but as many as received Him, to them He gave the right to become children of God" (Jn 1:12). For those who possess the pearl and wear it, live and reign with Christ forever as kings, as it is written,

"to Him who loved us and washed us from our sins in His own blood, and has made us kings and priests to His God and Father, to Him be glory and dominion forever and ever" (Rev 1:5-6).

For this reason, the apostle said "as we have borne the image of the man of dust, we shall also bear the image of the heavenly Man" (1 Cor 15:49). He also said "put on the Lord Jesus Christ, and make no provision for the flesh, to fulfil its lusts" (Rom 13:14).

The Holy Spirit tames our wild souls to be useful heavenly citizens

2. The Holy Spirit works with us like men working with wild horses to tame them. Wild horses are not useful to people if they are not tamed. For them to become reasonable and beneficial, men work patiently and consistently with them to train them to accept a new way of living. Likewise, the Holy Spirit patiently and consistently works with us, in our minds and hearts, to make us useful members of the royal family of God and citizens of heaven. Since sin entered into human minds and hearts, human souls became unruly and only interested in the company of other rowdy spirits, which are the devil and his people. But, when the soul hears the word of God, believes in truth and becomes bridled by the Holy Spirit, the soul casts off all the worldly desires and earthly cares. Soon afterwards, the soul goes through difficult times, sufferings and chastening for its honor and purification. As Jesus rides on those wild souls (see Homily 1), He gradually tames the soul, making it a dwelling place for the Holy Spirit. Consequently, sin and its powers fade away from those tamed souls especially when He arms them with the breastplate of righteousness, the helmet of salvation, the shield of faith

and the sword of the Spirit (Eph 6:14-17). Then those souls are taught to wage a spiritual war against the real enemies "to quench all the fiery darts of the wicked one" (Eph 6:16). As the faithful souls obtains those spiritual weapons of the Holy Spirit, they experience severe wars and sufferings, but only by crying out to the Lord they defeat the enemies. And so, having fought the war and shared in the victory with the help of the Holy Spirit, the soul receives crowns of victory with great glory as Saint Paul said

> "finally, there is laid up for me the crown of righteousness, which the Lord, the righteous Judge, will give to me on that Day, and not to me only but also to all who have loved His appearing" (2 Tim 4:8).

Prayer: My Lord, I trust that You will tame my rowdy soul so that it departs from all the powers of darkness and instead comes to be united with You, until I become worthy to put on the jewel of Your Holy Spirit that makes me a member of Your royal family. Guide me as You guide Your chariot in the direction You wish, whenever You wish. Help me to persevere in Your way, fighting the good fight, till I receive the Crown of Life from Your unblemished hands.

To Him be glory and honor forever. Amen.

Chapter 17

The Yeast

Homily 24: Our Lord Jesus taught that "the kingdom of heaven is like a merchant seeking beautiful pearls, who, when he had found one pearl of great price, went and sold all that he had and bought it" (Mt 13:45-46).

The great trade
    1. Like good traders who collect earthly profits from all their different enterprises to prepare for a better deal, true Christians collect their thoughts and bring back the focus of their life to their Lord. This is how they gain eternal life and a better reward with the help of the Holy Spirit. This world stands in contrast to the world above, and this age is pitted against the age to come. Therefore, it is necessary that true Christians deny the world by lifting their minds out of this present age. They need to lay aside the concerns of this world as Saint Paul said "be transformed by the renewing of your mind" (Rom 12:2) and, "set your mind on things above, not on things on the earth" (Col 3:2). Our minds and hearts must be

redirected to live in the world above, which is the world of the Holy Trinity. It is said "our citizenship is in heaven" (Phil 3:20) and Christians cannot attain this unless they deny this world. When Christians believe wholeheartedly in the Lord, the power of the Spirit of God gathers their hearts and minds together, bringing them into submission to the Lord who lovingly prepares their souls for eternal life.

The yeast of the Holy Spirit or the yeast of evil desires

2-4. Since Adam fell, peoples' thoughts have moved away from the love of God towards the love of this world, and they have become mingled with absurd and earthly interests. After Adam transgressed God's commandment, he took on the yeast of evil passions, and ever since then, the whole race of Adam shares with him in that tendency to do evil, whenever each person participates in sin. It has become like yeast working its way through each person's soul. That evil yeast is an image of Satan's power over peoples' spirits and their intellect. As it has grown and increased in people, their sinful desires have developed into corruptions, sexual immorality, pride, the love of worldly possessions and other absurd things until mankind has become permeated with the yeast of evil. As that yeast of evil desires has continued to grow in people, they have not been able to perceive God and have consequently denied His existence.

> "And even as they did not like to retain God in their knowledge, God gave them over to a debased mind, to do those things which are not fitting; being filled with all unrighteousness, sexual immorality, wickedness, covetousness, maliciousness; full of envy, murder, strife, deceit, evil-mindedness; they are

whisperers, backbiters, haters of God, violent, proud, boasters, inventors of evil things, disobedient to parents, undiscerning, untrustworthy, unloving, unforgiving, unmerciful; who, knowing the righteous judgment of God, that those who practice such things are deserving of death, not only do the same but also approve of those who practice them" (Rom 1:28-32).

In a similar way the Lord, who was pleased to suffer on behalf of all of us, came to our world to put His heavenly yeast of goodness into the souls of His faithful people. He is very pleased to work with us "till we all come to the unity of the faith and of the knowledge of the Son of God, to a perfect man, to the measure of the stature of the fullness of Christ" (Eph 4:13). We become united with Him in one Spirit as Saint Paul declared that; "he who is joined to the Lord is one spirit with Him" (1 Cor 6:17). In this mysterious unity with Him, we become completely permeated by the Spirit of God, just as yeast works its way through all the dough to cause it to rise. As a result of this, all those evil desires and ungodly thoughts do not enter our souls again and we become like the person who is filled with divine love, who; thinks no evil (1 Cor 13:5). But without the heavenly yeast, which is the power of the Spirit of God, it is not possible that a person can be permeated with the goodness of the Lord and thus have eternal life. When the Lord puts this yeast of the Holy Spirit in the race of Adam, people are not seduced again by such evil and wickedness unless the yeast of evil, which is sin, creeps into them.

Take the example of a person kneading flour without putting leaven into it. Regardless of how much effort he puts in to turn it over and over and thoroughly working it, the lump of dough will still remain unleavened and unfit to be made bread. But if leaven is put into the dough, it spreads throughout the whole mass of dough and leavens it all (causes it to rise). The Lord described this in His parable about the kingdom: "The kingdom of heaven is like leaven, which a woman took and hid in three measures of meal till it was all leavened" (Mt 13:33). The whole of mankind is like unleavened dough.

But the holy leaven belongs to another world; it is the divine nature of the Holy Spirit. If, therefore, the heavenly leaven of the Spirit (that is from another land) does not enter our lowly human nature, we remain unleavened and are not freed from the destructive state of evil. However, when the Holy Spirit fills us, we become leavened and useful as we are freed from all evil desires.

Without the Holy Spirit, we can achieve nothing

5,6. If anyone thinks that he or she can attain holiness alone without the help of the Holy Spirit, he or she is totally in error. For whatever people attempt to do by themselves, relying diligently on their own powers, will be done in vain, because such an attitude is not fit for the kingdom of Heaven "for it is God who works in you both to will and to do for His good pleasure" (Phil 2:13). Unless we approach God by denying the world, and believing with hope and patience that we will receive the power of the Holy Spirit (which is different from our own nature), we will never recover from the intoxication of materialism and worldly desires. Then we will never awake from the deepest sleep of ignorance in order to truly know Him as He is. Unless the Lord sends His divine life to us from above, we will never experience true eternal life.

It is indeed a "holy day" when the Spirit brightly illuminates the soul to make it shine, for unless a person is deemed worthy through faith to obtain grace, he or she is ineffective and unsuited for the Kingdom of God. But on the other hand, whoever receives the grace of the Spirit and does not turn away from negligence or wrongdoing, cannot participate in eternal life. This person resists grace and grieves the Spirit. For this reason, Saint Paul told us "do not grieve the Holy Spirit of God, by whom you were sealed for the day of redemption" (Eph 4:30). True Christians ought to demonstrate their acceptance of God's grace and power by their virtues, for example love, kindness, goodness, joy, simplicity, and divine gladness. In this way, we can become like Him in His goodness. Indeed, our free choice is tested by situations designed to help us to grow and progress in our journey towards Him. These situations show whether a person is continually united with the grace of God, until he or she gradually fully comes to be one with the Spirit. Then, he or she becomes holy and pure by the work of the Holy Spirit, and thus is made fit for the Kingdom of Heaven.

Prayer: My good shepherd, take away the leaven of evil passion from me and instead fill me with Your Holy Spirit that I will be leavened by You to be a new useful person fit for Your kingdom. Without You, I can do nothing. Please, make me "will" to live fully for You and "do" all the work that pleases You. Please support me so that I never grieve Your Holy Spirit again through my laziness, negligence or wrongdoing. Make me one with You as You have planned for me.

Glory and adoration to the undefiled Father and to the Holy Spirit forever. Amen.

Chapter 18

Honor of Unity

Homily 26: On the dignity and value of the immortal soul. How we can obtain the freedom of the Holy Spirit despite Satan's frequent temptations.

The precious value of the immortal soul
    1. Beloved, you must know that your intellectual soul has been given very much honor and dignity, and is considered by God to be very lovely and worthy. He takes pleasure in choosing your soul as His dwelling place, instead of the whole heavens and earth. Therefore, your immortal soul is like a precious vessel for the Holy Spirit. Look how great the heavens and the earth are, yet God did not take pleasure in them, but in you. He died for you, not for the angels or for any of the heavenly hosts. When you were lost and wounded by sin, the Lord came to your aid in order to call you back. He restored you to a state of purity, like Adam when he was first created. At that time, Adam was a lord over the heavens and the earth. He was pure, without any sin or evil, as he was

made in the likeness of God. However, by this transgression he was lost and was wounded. Though Satan darkened his mind, mankind was still alive, possessing a will that can differentiate good from evil.

Adam the second is better than Adam the first

2. *Question:* Is it true that when the Holy Spirit fills the soul that lust and sin are totally uprooted?

Answer: When a person is filled with the Holy Spirit, both sin and lust are uprooted as that person receives again the original pure state in which Adam was created at the beginning. Moreover, by the power of the Spirit and the renewal of the mind, this person does not just measure up to the first Adam, but surpasses him to reach a greater state, for we become "partakers of the divine nature" (2 Pet 1:14).

> "Therefore, just as through one man sin entered the world, and death through sin, and thus death spread to all men, because all sinned— (For until the law sin was in the world, but sin is not imputed when there is no law. Nevertheless, death reigned from Adam to Moses, even over those who had not sinned according to the likeness of the transgression of Adam, who is a type of Him who was to come. But the free gift is not like the offense. For if by the one man's offense many died, much more the grace of God and the gift by the grace of the one Man, Jesus Christ, abounded to many. And the gift is not like that which came through the one who sinned. For the judgment which came from one offense resulted in condemnation, but the free gift which came from many offences resulted in justification. For if by the one man's offense death reigned through the one, much more those who

receive abundance of grace and of the gift of righteousness will reign in life through the One, Jesus Christ.) Therefore, as through one man's offense judgment came to all men, resulting in condemnation, even so through one Man's righteous act the free gift came to all men, resulting in justification of life. For as by one man's disobedience many were made sinners, so also by one Man's obedience many will be made righteous" (Rom 5:12-19).

Prayer: My Lord fill me with Your Holy Spirit who will take away my sins and uproot all my deep-seated lust. Restore to me the image You created me in, Your image, so that I may grow in Your grace to be fully united with You. It is truly amazing how You convert my sins into justification by Your love through Your Holy Spirit.

Temptations are only allowed in limited measures for our benefits
3,4,7,8. *Question*: Can Satan war against us as he wishes, or has God put certain limits on him that he cannot exceed?
Answer: Satan attacks not only Christians but also all the unbelievers in the whole world. Therefore, if he was allowed to wage war as he wished, he would destroy all human beings, for this is his original desire.

Just as the potter controls the oven temperature to achieve the best quality for his pots, and like the goldsmith who expertly wields fire to fashion the best jewelry, it follows that God limits the enemy's power much more than that. God knows what sort of vessels humans are, so He only permits the enemy to have a limited measure of power. God knows how much each person is able to be a good steward, and gives him or her various gifts accordingly. That is clear in the book of Job, as Satan was unable to do anything by himself without permission from God. The devil said to the Lord; "stretch out Your hand now, and touch his bone and his flesh, and he will surely curse You to Your face!" (Job 2:5) and the Lord said to Satan; "Behold, all that he has is in your power; only do not lay a hand on his person" (Job 1:12). However, Job did not move away from his righteous ways. Therefore, as far as a person seeks God's help and is eager to receive His grace, Satan desires to tempt him. In fact, he said to the Lord

> "Does Job fear God for nothing? Have You not made a hedge around him, around his household, and around all that he has on every side? You have blessed the work of his hands, and his possessions have increased in the land. But now, stretch out Your hand and touch all that he has, and he will surely curse You to Your face!" (Job 1:9-11).

Occasionally, while a person is comforted in his journey with God, God could withdraw His grace from him or her and he or she could be delivered up to temptations. The devil comes, bringing multiple waves of negative feelings, experiences and thoughts such as despair, pain, troubles, fears and evil thoughts in an attempt to weaken the soul in order to alienate it from God so that it no longer hopes. Nevertheless, the prudent person does not give up hope, instead he or she holds onto the promises of God and as much as the devil brings against him or her, he or she endures in the face of all dangers and temptations, saying even if I die, I shall "not let him go" (Song 3:4). Then, if a person endures faithfully to the end, the Lord begins to converse with Satan saying "you see how many evils and afflictions you have inflicted on him and yet he has not obeyed you, but he continues to serve Me and fear Me." Satan is then overcome by shame and has nothing further to say. In the case of Job, if the devil had known that Job would remain faithful despite temptation and would not be conquered, he would certainly never have desired to try to make him fall, out of fear of being humiliated. So also, now, in the case of those who bear afflictions and temptations, Satan is put to shame as he has attained nothing.

"Blessed is the man who endures temptation; for when he has been approved, he will receive the crown of life which the Lord has promised to those who love Him. Let no one say when he is tempted 'I am tempted by God,' for God cannot be tempted by evil nor does He Himself tempt anyone. But, each one is tempted when he is drawn away by his own desires and enticed. Then, when desire has conceived, it gives birth to sin; and sin, when it is full-grown, brings forth death. Do not be deceived, my beloved brethren. Every good gift and every perfect gift is from above, and comes down from the Father of lights, with whom there is no variation or shadow of turning" (Jm 1:12-17).

Prayer: Lord, when Satan attacks me with troubles, problems, failures, fears, negative thoughts, self-doubt or earthly desires, please remind me that it is all for my glory, and within the limits that You have set in Your mercy and love. Give me the power of the Holy Spirit to put Satan to shame and to always honor Your name.

The finishing line of our war with Satan

14. Question: Does Satan ever stop waging wars against us? Do people ever become free from the war?

Answer: Satan never gives up in his fight against

us. As long as a person lives in the flesh in this world, he or she is subject to Satan's wars. However, when "the fiery darts of the wicked one are quenched" (Eph 6:16), he can inflict no harm on people. If someone manages to become such a close friend of the king that none of the king's ranks of nobles dare to prevent him from reaching the king, then no adversary can stand against him. So also, true Christians who live in unity with God as "partakers of the divine nature" (2 Pet 1:4), fear no harm, even if they are attacked in war by Satan, as they are not only friends with God but also united with Him. The person "who is joined to the Lord is one spirit with Him" (1 Cor 6:17). Therefore, when they have put on the power that comes from above and entered the rest that is granted to them by the Lord they dearly love, they will be saying with David, "the Lord is my light and my salvation; whom shall I fear? The Lord is the strength of my life; of whom shall I be afraid? (Ps 27:1).

    15,16,17. Just as the Lord put on a human body, leaving behind every heavenly principality and power, in a similar way Christians should also put on the Holy Spirit in order to find peace. Even if war starts externally as Satan attacks, they are still fortified internally by the Lord's power. Therefore, they are not anxious or worried about Satan. When Satan tempted the Lord in the wilderness for forty days, no harm came to Him. Although Satan attacked His body externally, he could do nothing to Him internally as He was God. So we Christians, may be tempted externally by Satan, nevertheless, internally we are filled with the Holy Trinity, therefore we suffer no harm. If someone has reached this level of spirituality, he or she has experienced the perfect love of Christ and the fullness of the Divine nature of God. But a person who is not at this level still struggles with interior wars, because at certain times he or she delights in prayer, but at other times he or she is bombarded by the afflictions of war. Since such a person is still an infant, the Lord trains him or her in war like a father trains his own son to defend himself. It is like two opposing forces; light and darkness; rest and affliction. Do you not hear what Saint Paul says?

> "Though I speak with the tongues of men and of angels, but have not love, I have become sounding brass or a clanging cymbal. And though I have the gift of prophecy, and understand all mysteries and all knowledge, and though I have all faith, so that I could remove mountains, but have not love, I am nothing. And though I bestow all my goods to feed the poor, and though I give my body to be burned, but have not love, it profits me nothing" (1 Cor 13:1-3).

For these gifts are not our aims but instead they are given to us to encourage us to reach that high and satisfying level of the knowledge of the fullness of God. Those who settle for lesser things are still infants, even though they live in the light. For many of the brothers have reached a degree of spirituality and enjoyed the gifts of healing and prophecy, but because they did not reach the "bond of perfection" (Col 3:14), when war came on them and they fell because they were negligent. But if anyone does reach that perfect bond, he or she is bound and taken into the deep fully captive by grace. If anyone somewhat approaches this level of perfection, yet does not succeed in being completely bound by grace, that person is still fearful of war and prone to the possibility of falling. Unless he or she is strengthened in the Lord, Satan will always try to overthrow him or her. This is how many who have been given grace went astray and lost that grace because they thought that they had obtained perfection while they were still far from it.

The Lord neither has limits nor is He totally comprehensible. No Christians can dare to claim "to have apprehended" (Phil 3:13) this goal of knowing Him, but they are humble, night and day, in their search for His incomprehensible mercies. In this uncertain world, there is no end to learning and education. No one appreciates this better than a person who has begun to learn. In the country of the illiterate, the one who is half educated is called the most learned person and praised as the wisest man in that place. However, if the same person journeys to a great city where there are truly learned people and scholars, he will not dare to speak up in front of them, in case the scholars judge him as an illiterate man. Certainly, the more you learn, the more you know that you do not know much at all. So in this case also, God is incomprehensible to man and He cannot be measured. Those who have begun to taste Him, and acknowledged their own weakness, know this very well. This is well illustrated in the book of Revelation where God is described in the new heaven:

> "His eyes were like a flame of fire, and on His head were many crowns. He had a name written that no one knew except Himself. He was clothed with a robe dipped in blood, and His name is called The Word of God" (Rev 19:12-13).

Prayer: My Lord, I am still in my infancy, forgive my arrogance that one day I imagined that I could comprehend You or fully understand Your ways. Help me to grow to achieve the "bond of perfection" in Your grace, so that I will overcome the devil and never fall by negligence or arrogance on my way to Your kingdom. As You put on a human body to reach out to me, let me put on

You and be filled with Your Holy Spirit that I may reach out to You.

God accepts us all regardless of our personalities

5,6. *Question*: Does the Holy Spirit change the personalities and characters of those who accept Him?

Answer: The personality remains the same; strong in a strong person, and easy going in an easy-going person. Nonetheless God accepts us all and works in us all regardless of our personalities. It happens that an uneducated person may be reborn spiritually and change to become very wise, but is still uneducated. Another person is rough by nature, but then when he willfully puts all his life in the Lord's hands, God accepts him, but the roughness of his nature persists and yet God is pleased with him. Another person who is kind and gentle by nature offers himself to God and the Lord accepts him. However, if he does not persevere in good works, God is not pleased with him. In order that God may manifest His compassion, He accepts every sort of personality and every kind of people, with varying dispositions. The whole nature of mankind is changeable for good or for evil. For if people desire, they have the power to carry out evil or good. When you write something unintentionally on a blank sheet of paper, you erase it. So also, determined people who give their wills over to God can be accepted by Him.

The apostles had different personalities. They would have wanted to give life to all the dead and to bring health to all the sick, and yet they did not always have their own way that seemed ideal or perfect, but only did what was permitted. For instance, when Paul was captured by the governor of Damascus, he could have arranged for the governor and the wall to be toppled, if the grace that was in him had desired it, since he was a man who possessed the Holy Spirit. However, the apostle was let down in a basket (2 Cor 11:30-33). You might wonder why he did not use the divine power that was in him. These things happened, so that in some cases they performed signs and wonders, but in other cases their human weakness was obvious in order that the faith of the believers may distinguish them from the unbelievers. It was an opportunity for them to demonstrate their free will and to demonstrate whether or not some of them would be offended by having a weaker side. For if the apostles had accomplished everything they wished, they would have brought people and their free will into God's service by a certain compulsory force and not by faith or by unbelief. Christianity is "a stumbling stone and rock of offense" (Rom 9:33).

Can Satan read my mind and influence my thought process?

9. *Question*: Does Satan know all the thoughts and plans of man?

Answer: No, but he observes and assumes. If you are friendly with other people and know things concerning them, you can predict how your friends will think and react. If you, who are possibly twenty years old or so, know things concerning your friends, family members and neighbors, why would Satan not understand your tendencies and infer your intentions as he has been observing you since you were born? For he has already been dealing with the human race since Adam fell from grace. Yet still he does not know exactly what a person intends or plans to do. For the tempter tempts, but he does not know whether a person will obey him or not until the person gives up his or her will as a slave. The devil does not know all the thoughts of a person's heart and its desires. The human mind has many domains and attributes like a tree that has many branches and fruits. Satan can grasp some of them, but by no means can he manage to grasp or influence all of the domains, intentions and deep-seated characteristics of a person.

We will defeat Satan with hope and joy
10,11,12. The mind produces thoughts and intentions, and sometimes evil takes the upper hand, but at other times people's good thoughts remain superior to those evil influences as they receive help and deliverance from God while resisting evil. Occasionally, a person is overcome by evil, but on other occasions he or she shows a strong and pure will to overcome all evil. When Satan observes a person rebelling against him and running passionately to God, he tries to bring him or her back to his or her dark ways. But he is incapable of restraining him or her when the person has a genuine desire to reach out to God and to be united with Him. For people have a natural tendency to love God, believe in Him, seek Him and come to Him.

In the material world of things around us, as the farmer works the soil and waits for rain, so also in the spiritual world there are two elements required. It is necessary for people to work the soil of their hearts through their free will and hard work. While God looks at people's hard work, toil and labor, He sends the heavenly rain of the Holy Spirit to nurture growth. However, if the heavenly clouds from above do not appear to bring down the showers of grace, the farmer will achieve nothing despite all his or her hard work and knowledge of farming. This is the sign of Christianity; however much a person does and however many justifying works he or she performs, the true Christian should always feel that he or she has accomplished nothing. When he or she fasts, he or she should say "I have not fasted yet." When he or she prays, let him or her think "I have not prayed yet. I have only begun to practice fasting and prayers."

As the Lord said "when you have done all those things which you are commanded, say, 'We are unprofitable servants. We have done what was our duty to do'" (Lk 17:10). And even if someone is righteous before God, he or she must say: "I am not righteous. I am not laboring enough, but I begin each day." Every day he or she ought to have hope in the future kingdom and in the redemption of his or her soul, reassuring himself or herself with humility, joy and confidence that "If today I have not gained deliverance, tomorrow I will." It is like a man who plants a vineyard, who works every day in hope and joy as he ponders in his mind the profit of his vineyards, even though there is no wine yet. In this way, he puts himself to work every day in hope and good expectation, toiling with joy even if sometimes he pays a great expense out of his own pocket. It is like someone who builds a house or cultivates a field. At first, he invests in his project in the hope of future profits. It is the same way in this matter. Unless the person keeps joy and hope before his or her eyes, telling himself or herself confidently "I shall obtain salvation and life," he or she cannot easily accept the journey along the narrow road. For it is the presence of hope and joy that allows him or her to labor and to bear the burden of traveling along the narrow path. The Bible says that while "rejoicing in hope, patient in tribulation, continuing steadfastly in prayer" (Rom 12:12), we all must work out our "own salvation with fear and trembling" (Phil 2:12), in order to be worthy to not "fall into reproach and the snare of the devil" (1 Tim 3:7). As athletes train hard to win worldly honor in the Olympics, we also must work hard to be deemed worthy of the honor of the saints, as

Saint Paul said; "Do you not know that those who run in a race all run, but one receives the prize? Run in such a way that you may obtain it. And everyone who competes for the prize is temperate in all things. Now they do it to obtain a perishable crown, but we for an imperishable crown. Therefore, I run thus: not with uncertainty. Thus, I fight: not as one who beats the air" (1 Cor 9:24-26).

The purity of the soul
13. If you keep your body outwardly free from sin and uncleanness, but inwardly commit adultery and lust in your thoughts, you are an adulterer before God. As the Lord said; "whoever looks at a woman to lust for her has already committed adultery with her in his heart" (Mt 5:28). Physical virginity profits you nothing if you are unfaithful in your heart to the Lord your God who said "I am married to you" (Jr 3:14). If a bride was enticed by another man and committed sexual immorality, her husband might loathe her for the act she did. So also, the spiritual soul that accepts any partnership with Satan (the serpent that lies in hiding in the interior recesses) commits adultery with the evil spirit against God. In the same way "friendship with the world is enmity with God" (Jm 4:4). This soul is then deemed unfaithful to the Lord and will have no place with the hundred and forty-four thousand who shall stand in white with the Lamb on Mount Zion singing the new song (Rev 14:1-3), for they did not defile themselves with Satan or his darkness. For there is a sin committed through the body, and yet another kind of sin committed in fellowship with Satan. The same soul can either be a partner of demons or of God and His angels. If it commits spiritual adultery with the devil, it is inadequate to be a partner of the heavenly Bridegroom. On the other hand,

repentance makes harlots virgins again as they resume their unity with God who calls us all to salvation and restores us to His own image.

Your soul will follow your real love
18. *Question*: If a man is engaged in this interior war but still entertains both good and evil desires (namely, he has both sin and grace) then he departs from this world, where does his soul go, since he has been entertaining those two opposing principles?

Answer: The mind goes where it finds its goal and the soul follows its love. For the fact that war comes on you is not your doing, however, it is up to you to hate it and to reject evil desires. Then the Lord, seeing the determination of your mind, that you are struggling and that you love Him with your whole soul, drives death away from your soul and receives you in His arms, into His light. In a flash, God snatches you from the jaws of darkness and immediately takes you into His kingdom. For God, all things are easily accomplished, if only you show your love for Him. God wants to see peoples' free will at work, since the human soul is meant to have fellowship with the Holy Trinity.

No fruit without the Holy Spirit
19, 20. We have already often spoken about the parable of the farmer who works and throws seed on the earth. Unless he receives heavenly rain from above, the work of the farmer achieves nothing. In the same way, if someone relies only on his or her own efforts and does not receive the grace of the Holy Spirit, he or she cannot produce fruit, which is worthy of the Lord.

> "Therefore brethren, be patient until the coming of the Lord. See how the farmer waits for the precious fruit of the earth, waiting patiently for it

until it receives the early and latter rain" (Jm 5:7).

The work of men and women is to renounce the world, to persevere in prayer and to love God and all people. It is up to humans to labor continuously, but if they endure in their work and do not seek a material reward in this world, and only wish to please God and to become one with Him, then the winds of the Holy Spirit will blow on their souls and the heavenly clouds will bring rain to nurture these souls so that they will give the Lord fruit that is worthy of Him. It is written; "Every branch in Me that does not bear fruit He takes away; and every branch that bears fruit He prunes, that it may bear more fruit" (Jn 15:2). When someone does any good work, he or she should attribute it all to the Lord, and say; "If God had not empowered me, I could never have fasted or prayed or left the world." In this way, God sees your good intention, that you ascribe to God all the things that you accomplish, and He gives you those things that are from Him, namely, the spiritual, divine and heavenly things, which are the fruit of the Spirit. "The fruit of the Spirit is love, joy, peace, longsuffering, kindness, goodness, faithfulness, gentleness, self-control. Against such there is no law" (Gal 5:22-23).

21,22. The fruit that comes out of our own nature such as kindness, faith and love is different from the spiritual fruit of the Holy Spirit. The things you accomplish of yourself are good and acceptable to God, but they are not pure or perfect. For example, you may love God, but your love will not be perfect until the Lord comes and gives you heavenly love, which is unchangeable and selfless. You pray naturally with anxiety and with thoughts that distract you till God gives you the gift of pure prayer that is in spirit and truth (Jn 4:23). It is like a farmer who roots out the weeds from the earth and digs up the thorns, but then they come up again and again despite his diligent work, just as in the days of Adam, who was told "both thorns and thistles it shall bring forth for you" (Gen 3:18). After the fall of Adam, the soil of the human heart produced thistles and thorns. Though a person takes pain to tend the soil frequently, the thorns of evil spirits still spring up, until the Holy Spirit Himself helps in our weaknesses (Rom 8:26) and the Lord plants heavenly seed in the soil of the heart and cultivates it. Though the holy seed has fallen into the soil, thistles and thorns still spring up. Only when the Lord Himself expertly tills the soil of the soul with His abundant grace, then the thistles dry up from the heat of the Sun of Righteousness (Mal 4:2) and the fruit of the Spirit appears in the lives of true Christians. As the Holy Spirit continues His work with the obedient soul, then the evil that still exists in the soul, loses the dominance it previously held. This is like wheat blades that become stronger, so that the weeds that used to choke them have no power over them anymore. When the gift of God and His grace fill someone abundantly so that he or she is rich in the Lord, then evil has no power to greatly harm that person. Even if evil is present to some degree, the evil forces do not have any power to control him or her.

The Lord's purpose in coming to Earth is to free those who have been held captive by evil and to make them conquerors over death and sin. Therefore, you should not think it strange if certain people give you trouble, as it encourages you to struggle against such evil.

> "Beloved, do not think it strange concerning the fiery trial which is to try you, as though some strange thing happened to you; but rejoice to the extent that you partake of Christ's sufferings, that when His glory is revealed, you may also be glad with exceeding joy" (1 Pet 4:12-13).

Prayer: My Lord, work with my soul in Your grace and pour Your Holy Spirit on me so that I may receive Your gifts of true love, spiritual prayers and acceptable fasting. Make Your Sun of Righteousness shine on me and destroy all the weeds of sin and evil. Give me the strength to persevere in prayers and renounce the love of the world for without Your rain and help, I will never be fruitful or useful.

As He suffered for us, we ought to suffer for Him

23, 24. No one is immune from falling, because we have free will that can choose good or evil. Even those who are perfect should be very careful, as long as they live in the flesh, in case they fall. The obedient soul suffers opposition, like the ancient prophets who were wronged by people from their own nation. In the new church, we have been given the baptism of fire, which is the circumcision of the heart and the heavenly Holy Spirit dwelling in our minds. But as long as people are stricken with fear, they would be tempted. Therefore, A person can only live without afflictions and temptations once he or she reaches the city of the saints; "the holy city, New Jerusalem, coming down out of heaven from God" (Rev 21:2). For in the Lord's eternal city, there will be no more worry or afflictions or labor or tears or Satan, but only rest, joy, peace and salvation.

> "Behold, the tabernacle of God is with men, and He will dwell with them, and they shall be His people. God Himself will be with them and be their God. And God will wipe away every tear from their eyes; there shall be no more death, nor sorrow, nor crying. There shall be no more pain, for the former things have passed away" (Rev 21:3-4).

The Lord is among them who is the Savior, because He sets the captives free. He is called Physician because His heavenly, divine medicine heals the soul. Jesus is the King of kings and Lord of lords (Rev 19:16), but Satan is a tyrant and an evil ruler. God and His angels wish to make everyone a member of the heavenly family in their kingdom. Likewise, the devil and his angels also wish to adopt people as their own. The human soul is caught between these two powers.

Eventually the soul belongs to the power it chooses; either God or Satan. For example, a father who sends his son into a foreign land provides him with medicines and remedies in case he is attacked by animals, snakes or diseases along the way. So also, we should strive to receive heavenly medicine from God our Father. He gives us a healing antidote for the soul, so that we may use it to kill the poisonous wild beasts, which are the unclean spirits. For it is not easy to maintain a pure heart without great effort and work. A person can only obtain a clear conscience and a clean heart by putting to work all the remedies and treatments given by God, in order that evil may be completely uprooted.

25. All the just people who have pleased God, have persevered in righteousness on the narrow way to the end without ever letting their guard down. Abraham still considered himself to be "dust and ashes" (Gen 18:27) even though he was rich both in the eyes of God and of the world. David also said; "But I am a worm, and no man; a reproach of men, and despised by the people" (Ps 22:6). On the other hand, people who fell back into sin after they had been visited by grace did so because they did not realize that grace and sin could co-exist, like smoke and fire, each trying to influence the same heart. The Lord gives healing medicines to heal all the

wounded, as Isaiah said "He was wounded for our transgressions, He was bruised for our iniquities; the chastisement for our peace was upon Him, and by His stripes we are healed" (Is 53:5).

26. If even Jesus appeared outwardly poor and humiliated like one of us, we should not ever despise His Divine glory, because for our sakes He appeared on earth in a common, simple human body. Consider how He was humiliated more than all men at the hour when the crowd gathered against Him and cried out "Crucify Him, crucify Him" (Lk 23:21). And what more humiliation could He have undergone after they spat in His face and placed a crown of thorns on Him and slapped Him? For it is written that; "I gave My back to those who struck Me, and My cheeks to those who plucked out the beard; I did not hide My face from shame and spitting" (Is 50:6). If God accepts such insults and sufferings and humiliation, we, who by nature are made of earthly matter and are mortal, will never experience anything similar to our Lord no matter how much we are humiliated. God humbled Himself for our sake, so how can we refuse to be humbled for our own sakes? However, most of the time, we remain self-centered, proud and inflated. He came to take our afflictions and sufferings on Himself and to grant us His rest. Yet we often refuse to bear any difficulties or suffering that will result in the healing of our wounds.

Let us give glory to His patience and long suffering forever. Amen.

Chapter 19

Know Yourself

Homily 27: Humans have been crowned with glory and honor. People choose their own way because they have free will.

The knowledge of your glory will humble you

1. O people, know your nobility and dignity. You are the brothers and sisters of Christ (Mk 3:35), the friends of the King (Song 5:16) and the bride of the heavenly Bridegroom (Rev 22:17). For the person who knows the dignity of his or her soul is also able to know the power and the mysteries of the Holy Trinity. This knowledge will only make people more humbled, for the light of God makes people see their fallen state and appreciate the work of God in them. As Jesus was glorified and sat at the right hand of the Father after He suffered on the cross (Acts 2:33), so it is also necessary for you to suffer with Him, to be crucified with Him, and thus to ascend to be seated with Him at the right hand of the Father as someone joined to the Body of Christ, for

He "raised us up together, and made us sit together in the heavenly places in Christ Jesus" (Eph 2:6). Therefore, we will reign with Him forever in that new world as His children and "if children, then heirs—heirs of God and joint heirs with Christ, if indeed we suffer with Him, that we may also be glorified together" (Rom 8:17).

The honor of those who fight against the evil power
2. Those who conquer the devil and overcome the obstacles of evil, reach the heavenly city, the new Jerusalem (Rev 21:10), which is full of peace and many good things, where the "church of the firstborn" and "the spirits of just men" (Heb 12:23) find their rest. Indeed, it is not just that the Bridegroom came to suffer and to be crucified while the bride, for whom the Bridegroom came, lives in worldly distraction. The soul that gives itself over to every worldly love is corrupted by its unfaithfulness to the Lord. Those who have accepted the partnership of sin by their own choice have given away their will to evil as they have made peace with Satan and gave up on resisting him. But those who experience thoughts of sin that they have not chosen, and then do not consent to those thoughts, nor take pleasure in them, or surrender to them, but oppose them in words and deeds, are far more noble and honorable in God's eyes than those who freely give their will over to the devil.

> "I find then a law, that evil is present with me, the one who wills to do good. For I delight in the law of God according to the inward man. But I see another law in my members, warring against the law of my mind, and bringing me into captivity to the law of sin which is in my members. O wretched man that I am! Who will deliver me from this body of death? I thank God—through Jesus Christ our Lord! (Rom 7:21-25).

Prayer: My Lord, You in Your great love for me gave me a free will to choose my path that leads to my destination. Please be my way, my door and my shepherd in my journey back to You. Please give me the wisdom to reject evil intentions and the courage to refuse all peer pressure with all its worldly temptations. I hand over my will to You. Bring my will into line with Your will as You work in me to change me into the new nature that is on Your image.

The Lord made us kings and priests to our God

3,4,5,6. The way God has been dealing with us is like a king who found a poor girl dressed in rags. As he could not take her in like that, he washed her and dressed her in elegant clothes and then introduced her to his royal court as his friend. This is how the Lord treated the wounded soul that He found stricken by the devil, at the right time, the time of love (Ezk 16:8). In the same manner, He gave us all His mysterious medicine to remove the shame of sin and clothed us with the glorious, royal, heavenly honor of the Holy Trinity. He placed a crown on our heads (Rev 2:10) and made us His partners at the royal table with joy and gladness (Lk 22:30). Therefore, those who are renewed by God are kings and lords as described in the revelation of Saint John; "He is Lord of lords and King of kings; and those who are with Him are called, chosen, and faithful" (Rev 17:14). Therefore, Christianity is not just a religion, it is a mystery and those who truly live in it always say "This is a great mystery" (Eph 5:32). But the mystery of Christianity is alien to this world.

My friend, acknowledge that you have been chosen with great honor to be royal and noble for; "you are a chosen generation, a royal priesthood, a holy nation, His own special people" (1 Pet 2:9). The visible glory and wealth of the earthly kings are perishable and pass away. But the kingdom and riches of God are divine, heavenly and full of glory that will never pass away or dissolve. For the true Christians reign together with the heavenly King as it is written "If we endure, we shall also reign with Him" (2 Tim 2:12). Though they are chosen and approved by God and see His love working in them, they regard themselves as worthless and the least in the whole world, for they are oblivious to what they have obtained. For the Holy Spirit comes and teaches them not to count their life dear to them (Acts 20:24), but rather to regard themselves as naturally dishonorable. And though they progress in the knowledge of God, they still regard themselves as if they know nothing. Being rich before God, they consider themselves poor, for humility is their weapon against the old serpent that tries to destroy them again with the disease of pride and arrogance that attacks those who are not well rooted in Christ.

The grace of the Holy Spirit protects us against pride and arrogance

7,8,12. Christianity is truly eating and drinking from the truth; eating and drinking on and on until you experience power and sanctification. It is one thing to speak about a delicious drink in words and it is another thing to go and draw some out from the very fountain and drink to your full satisfaction. Those who have experienced this praise God with King David saying, "because Your lovingkindness is better than life, my lips shall praise You. Thus, I will bless You while I live; I will lift up my hands in Your name. My soul shall be satisfied as with marrow and fatness, and my mouth shall praise You with joyful lips" (Ps 63:3-5). It is like a man who was very thirsty till he found satisfying drink but then, while he was drinking, someone came and temporarily took the drink away. For the Lord gives us a taste of His living water but does not give us it all at once in case we become puffed up with pride and lose our senses. God knows that our nature is weak, and that it is not good for us to be filled with grace very quickly before we are fully prepared for it. But when a person eagerly asks for that living water because he or she has already tasted it and experienced its mysterious and reviving effect, God gives His grace in abundance because it is He; "who gives to all liberally and without reproach" (Jm 1:5). It is like a very poor man who found a treasure of gold. He became so elated, beginning to shout out; "I found a treasure; I am rich," that his enemies came and took it all away as he lost the balance of his mind. Therefore, God first gives us a taste of His grace, and then when we come back asking for more, He fills us gradually and generously according to His prudence and wisdom. For the door opens to many who seek God, so that they may see the treasure. But just as they joyfully exclaim; "We have found treasure," He shuts the doors. They then begin to cry out: "we found the treasure and then we lost it again." In God's plan, grace withdraws so that we may seek it more diligently. And when we find it again, we cling to it and never let it go away. This is illustrated in the Bible for us in the book of the Song of Solomon (3: 1-4):

> "By night on my bed I sought the one I love; I sought him, but I did not find him. "I will rise now," I said, "and go about the city; in the streets and in the squares, I will seek the one I love." I sought him, but did not find him. The watchmen who go about the city found me; I said, "Have you seen the one I love?" Scarcely had I passed by

them, when I found the one I love. I held him and would not let him go, until I had brought him to the house of my mother, and into the chamber of her who conceived me."

You choose your spiritual path by your own free will

9,10. *Question*: How is it that some people fall after the grace of God has visited them?

Answer: This is because people have the free will to choose their own way and make their own decision even after God's grace has visited them. This grace is not extinguished or diminished, but peoples' free will and liberty is put to the test to see which way they tend to choose. This means that grace permits sin to be present, so that you can choose your own way freely. And then you draw near to the Lord by your free choice and beg for His grace to come to you. For it is written "do not quench the Spirit" (1 Thess 5:19). The Spirit cannot be extinguished; He is always light. But it is you who lose the Holy Spirit if you are neglectful and do not willingly cooperate with grace as it says "do not grieve the Holy Spirit of God, by whom you were sealed for the day of redemption" (Eph 4:30). You see that it is up to your own will and freedom of choice to honor the Holy Spirit and not to grieve Him. Even perfect Christians who only move towards what is good and righteous although they are tested by many evils, still have free will. Our human nature can move towards either good or evil as the opposing forces act by enticement, not by necessity. For grace did not prevent the apostles, who were brought to perfection by grace, from doing whatever they wished to do, even if it was not in keeping with that grace. For example, when Saint Peter was to be blamed (Gal 2:11), Saint Paul had to correct him! And Saint Paul, as spiritual as he was, freely engaged in a quarrel with Saint

Barnabas and they were both so sharp that they left each other (Acts 15:39). This same Paul says "you who are spiritual restore such a one in a spirit of gentleness, considering yourself lest you also be tempted" (Gal 6:1). You see, spiritual people are put to the test because their free will remains and their enemies harass them as long as they remain in this world.

11. *Question*: Were the apostles capable of sinning if they chose, or was the grace of God too powerful for their free will?

Answer: We cannot say that they were incapable of sinning because they dwelt in the light and possessed this grace. Also, we do not imply that the grace they had was weak. But what we say is that grace permits even spiritually perfect people to have free will and to enjoy the power of doing whatever they want and going wherever they want. And human nature itself, as it is weak, enjoys the power to turn away from good. Take the example of people who are fully armed with breastplates and other armor. In short, they are personally protected and enemies do not attack them. Or, should the enemies attack, it is within the free will of those people to either use those arms and to fight against the enemies and to be victorious repelling them, or to take the easy path and make peace with the enemies and give up fighting, even though they are wearing armor. Likewise, Christians who have put on heavenly armor, have perfect power from God, however they can, if they wish, make peace with Satan and no longer resist him. Or they can choose to remain the children of God and fight the good fight as Saint Paul advised Saint Timothy saying "fight the good fight of faith, lay hold on eternal life, to which you were also called" (1 Tim 6:12).

Passing from death to life

13. *Question*: When a person accepts grace, he or she passes from death to life. Is it possible for someone who lives in the light to entertain impure thoughts?

Answer: Saint Paul asks "are you so foolish? Having begun in the Spirit, are you now being made perfect by the flesh?" (Gal 3:3). Again, he says; "Put on the whole armor of God, that you may be able to stand against the wiles of the devil" (Eph 6:11). These texts speak of two different levels. One is the level where a person is after he or she put on armor and the other is the level where he or she is when warring against principalities and powers of darkness. Also, we read that we need to be active and use this armor: "above all, taking the shield of faith with which you will be able to quench all the fiery darts of the wicked one" (Eph 6:16).

> "For it is impossible for those who were once enlightened, and have tasted the heavenly gift, and have become partakers of the Holy Spirit, and have tasted the good word of God and the powers of the age to come, if they fall away, to renew them again to repentance, since they crucify again for themselves the Son of God, and put Him to an open shame" (Heb 6:4-6).

There are those who have been enlightened and have tasted the Lord and still fell. You see that people possess the free will to live in harmony with the Holy Spirit and also the free will to grieve Him. When someone takes up arms to go into battle and struggle against the enemy, then that person is enlightened and can wage war against the powers of darkness.

No one is too good not to fall into sin

14,15,16. *Question*: What does the apostle mean in this statement:

> "Though I speak with the tongues of men and of angels, but have not love, I have become sounding brass or a clanging cymbal. And though I have the gift of prophecy, and understand all mysteries and all knowledge, and though I have all faith, so that I could remove mountains, but have not love, I am nothing. And though I bestow all my goods to feed the poor, and though I give my body to be burned, but have not love, it profits me nothing" (1 Cor 13:1-3)?

Answer: It would be a big misunderstanding if this is understood to mean that being an apostle is nothing, for it is a great honor from heaven. But all other gifts are of little value when compared to perfect love. A person who possesses all the other spiritual gifts to some degree may fall into sin, but the person who possesses perfect love will not fall. I tell you this, that I have seen people who received all the spiritual gifts and participated in the life of the Holy Spirit, but, as they had not achieved perfect love, they fell. Some of them suffered persecution for the name of Christ and others gave up all their riches to become monks, but they fell as they became puffed up, seeking the glory of people. They failed to take care to fully obey the word of God. No one is so good that he or she will never fall into sin. Therefore, we all ought to be on guard all the days of our life.

Let us not hand over our vessel to our enemies

17,18,19. *Question*: What is the meaning of the phrase; "Eye has not seen, nor ear heard, nor have entered into the heart of man the things which God has prepared for those who love Him" (1 Cor 2:9)?

Answer: The great prophets and the kings of the Old Testament knew that the Savior was coming. But they did not know and they had not heard that He would suffer, be crucified, and would pour out His blood on the cross. Nor did it enter into their hearts that there would be a baptism of fire and of the Holy Spirit as Saint John said; "I indeed baptize you with water unto repentance, but He who is coming after me is mightier than I, whose sandals I am not worthy to carry. He will baptize you with the Holy Spirit and fire" (Mt 3:11). They would not have been able to even imagine that in the new church the Lord's flesh and blood will be offered as bread and wine, and that those who receive a portion of the visible bread would eat spiritually of the flesh of the Lord that forgives all sins and gives eternal life. As the Lord said "whoever eats My flesh and drinks My blood has eternal life, and I will raise him up at the last day" (Jn 6:54). They could not have even thought that the new Christians would receive the Paraclete who is the "power from on high" (Lk 24:49) and be filled with the Holy Trinity and that their souls would be penetrated by the Holy Spirit. The prophets and kings did not know this, nor did it even enter into the imagination of their hearts. But now Christians enjoy a richness in another way and they are seized with a desire for the Holy Spirit. But even though they enjoy this joy and consolation, they still fear and tremble (Phil 2:12), being concerned that they may fail to cooperate with the grace of God and so take a wrong step. It is like a man who had a precious treasure but had to travel through places where there were robbers. Even though he was happy about the wealth and the treasure he carried, he was afraid that the robbers might attack him and divest him of his treasure. He was like someone who was carrying his own body in his hands.

Look, as far as external things are concerned, all of us have renounced them and are like pilgrims without possessions, deprived of any fellowship with the world. But as the body gets ready for prayer, so the mind also should keep up with the body. As your body is a stranger to the world, so your mind also should be alienated from the world and never get tied up with matters of this world "for where your treasure is, there your heart will be also" (Mt 6:21). You need to examine what treasure you have in your mind. Is your mind totally centered on God or not? If it is not, you must ask yourself what is the obstacle that distracts you. The evil desires that exists in the mind come from Satan and his demons, who hold captive the mind and the soul of those who obey him. For the devil is very cunning and has many tricks and loopholes and all sorts of deceits. He captures the unoccupied lands of the soul and the thoughts and does not allow the soul to pray properly and to draw near to God. For human nature can have a relationship with the demons (the evil spirits) equally as well as it can with the angels and with the Holy Spirit. The soul can be the temple of Satan or the temple of the Holy Spirit. Now, examine yourself again. Whose temple are you, the dwelling place of God or of the devil? What treasure fills your heart? Is it the grace of God or the evil of Satan? Just as a house that has been filled with foul smells and dung, must be completely cleaned up and put in order and filled with every good fragrance and all kinds of treasure, so it is that the Holy Spirit may come instead of Satan and may find rest in the souls of Christians. "Little children, let no one deceive you. He who practices righteousness is righteous, just as He is righteous. He who sins is of the devil, for the devil has sinned from the beginning. For this purpose, the Son of God was manifested, that He might destroy the works of the devil. Whoever has been born of God does not sin, for His seed remains in him; and he cannot sin, because he has been born of God" (1 Jn 3:7-9).

Prayer: My Lord, I fail to fully comprehend Your love and Your gifts to me. What Jacob, Joseph, Daniel, David and Isaiah did not have or dare to imagine, You have given in the form of bread and wine for the forgiveness of all my sins and for eternal life with You. Help me to choose Your way and give all my soul, mind and heart to You and give my body as a dwelling place for You.

Not in an instant but through a special journey along the narrow road

20,21,22. You need to know that after hearing the word of God, a person does not immediately become a saint nor is he or she ranked among good people. If the mere acceptance of the word of God made people righteous without any labor, there would have been no need for Saint Paul to teach in Antioch that; "We must through many tribulations enter the kingdom of God" (Acts 14:22). If people came immediately to complete rest, perfection and holiness, the Lord would not have instructed us to

> "enter by the narrow gate; for wide is the gate and broad is the way that leads to destruction, and there are many who go in by it. Because narrow is the gate and difficult is the way which leads to life, and there are few who find it" (Mt 7:13-14).

But if you believe that people are fully saved and guaranteed their place in heaven just by accepting the word of God, you ignore these principles. That concept deprives humans of their free will and also denies the opposing power that is struggling against their minds.

Saint Paul illustrated this war against the power of darkness when he said "we do not wrestle against flesh and blood, but against principalities, against powers, against the rulers of the darkness of this age, against spiritual hosts of wickedness in the heavenly places" (Eph 6:12).

This is what we believe, that the person who hears the word needs to come to repentance as Saint Peter advised those who on hearing the word of God "were cut to the heart" (Acts 2:37) saying, "repent, and let every one of you be baptized in the name of Jesus Christ for the remission of sins" (Acts 2:38). Then, after this, through God's providence and guidance, they withdraw from the pleasure of this world putting off the old man and his conduct as Saint Paul said,

> "if indeed you have heard Him and have been taught by Him, as the truth is in Jesus: that you put off, concerning your former conduct, the old man which grows corrupt according to the deceitful lusts, and be renewed in the spirit of your mind, and that you put on the new man which was created according to God, in true righteousness and holiness" (Eph 4:21-24).

Then, the Holy Spirit takes each one into a journey of development and training in holiness and the tactics of spiritual war which is the struggle and conflict against Satan. And after a long race, the person who is trained is then victorious in the struggle to become a true Christian, as Saint Paul said,

> "do you not know that those who run in a race all run, but one receives the prize? Run in such a way that you may obtain it. And everyone who competes for the prize is temperate in all things. Now they do it to obtain a perishable crown, but

we for an imperishable crown" (1 Cor 9:24-25).

If anyone could be numbered among good people by merely hearing the word, without any work, then all those who first knew the Lord and then denied Him by their deeds and words would enter the kingdom of life. But they could not achieve this without an effort and without a struggle because the road is straight and narrow (Mt 7:14). We know that we must travel along this bumpy and difficult road and patiently endure afflictions in order to enter eternal life.

If it had been possible to succeed without any effort, Christianity would not have been "a stumbling stone and rock of offense" (Rom 9:33). There would have been no faith or disbelief. This would mean that people were made slaves again, unable to choose to go in a good or evil direction. Satan has power to exhort and entice someone to follow his will, and yet the person has equal power to resist this and not to obey him at all. The powers of both evil and of good act by persuasion and not by force. Divine assistance is given to people who have this free choice and so people are able, as they battle, to receive heavenly armor and to use this to conquer and uproot sin. It is within the power of people to resist sin, even though they cannot conquer evil and uproot it without God.

Free will is the main attribute that remains with humans for all their lives and makes them capable of choosing life or death.

> "See, I have set before you today life and good, death and evil, in that I command you today to love the Lord your God, to walk in His ways, and to keep His commandments, His statutes, and His judgments, that you may live and multiply; and the Lord your God will bless you in the land which

you go to possess. But if your heart turns away so that you do not hear, and are drawn away, and worship other gods and serve them, I announce to you today that you shall surely perish" (Deut 30:15-18).

For the law is only given to a person who is capable of turning both ways, that is to someone who possesses the free will to do battle against the opposing force. You see, if you say that a person cannot change, you mean that a good person is unworthy of praise. For a person who is gentle and good by nature does not deserve praise, even if he or she may desire it. Good which is not freely chosen is not worthy of praise, even if praise seems desirable. Only the person who freely chooses to diligently struggle in the battle against evil and who embraces good is worthy of praise.

The road to God
23. The foundation of the road towards God requires patience, hope, humility, an attitude of poverty, gentleness and a determination to travel along the narrow road of life. This is how a person can receive justification from the Lord. Of course, by justification, we mean that the person receives the Lord Himself. These commandments are like milestones and signposts along the royal highway that leads the traveler to the heavenly city. For our Lord said

> "Blessed are the poor in spirit, for theirs is the kingdom of heaven. Blessed are those who mourn, for they shall be comforted. Blessed are the meek, for they shall inherit the earth. Blessed are those who hunger and thirst for righteousness, for they shall be filled. Blessed are the merciful, for they shall obtain

mercy. Blessed are the pure in heart, for they shall see God. Blessed are the peacemakers, for they shall be called sons of God. Blessed are those who are persecuted for righteousness' sake, for theirs is the kingdom of heaven. Blessed are you when they revile and persecute you, and say all kinds of evil against you falsely for My sake. Rejoice and be exceedingly glad, for great is your reward in heaven, for so they persecuted the prophets who were before you" (Mt 5:3-12).

This is what I call Christianity. Therefore, if anyone does not pass along this road, he has wandered off on an untrodden way.

May the mercy of the Father, the Son and the Holy Spirit be glorified forever. Amen.

Chapter 20

Birth From Above
Homily 30

Like father, like children
1,2. Those who hear the word of God should take note of the work of the word in their own souls. The word of God is not idle, it has its own effective work on the soul, fFor the word of God is living and powerful, and sharper than any two-edged sword, piercing even to the division of soul and spirit, and of joints and marrow, and is a discerner of the thoughts and intents of the heart" (Heb 4:12). For this reason, it is called a "work," so that its effect may be found in those who hear it. May the Lord, therefore, grant the work of truth to those who hear Him, so that His word may become effective in us, as the Lord said, "you are already clean because of the word which I have spoken to you" (Jn 15:3). For just as the shadow precedes the body, but reveals it, so also, while the truth is the body itself, the word is like a shadow of the truth of Christ. Thus, the word precedes the truth; accepting

the word of God comes first, then Christ dwells in our hearts in truth. Truly Jesus said "My Father has been working until now, and I have been working" (Jn 5:17).

Fathers beget children of their own nature from their body and soul, and carefully educate them attentively until they become full-grown men and women, for the aim of the earthly fathers from the beginning is to raise children in their image (Gen 1:27). In the same way also, our Lord Jesus Christ is always concerned with our salvation. God planned carefully from the beginning to bring us to Himself through the fathers, the patriarchs, the Law and the prophets. Finally, He himself came and suffered the shame of the cross and endured death. He took great care to create us from Himself and from his very own nature, so we are children of His Spirit. He was pleased with His plan that we should be born from above. And just as some fathers who have no descendants are saddened, so the Lord who loves mankind is also sad when anyone does not wish to be born from the womb of the Holy Spirit in His image. But, if any of us do not wish to experience such a birth and to be born from the womb of the Spirit of the Holy Trinity, Christ endures suffering on their behalf in order to save them.

The birth from above in His image
3. The Lord "desires all men to be saved and to come to the knowledge of the truth" (1 Tim 2:4) wishes all people to be worthy of this birth. As He died on behalf of us all, He has called all of us to live a new life through this birth from God. Without this birth, one cannot live as the Lord says "unless one is born again, he cannot see the Kingdom of God" (Jn 3:3). All who believe the Lord and come to Him, requesting Him to make them worthy to receive this birth, bring joy and great happiness in

Heaven to the Holy Trinity who gave birth to them. And all the angels and holy hosts rejoice over a person who is born of the Spirit and has become spiritual as the scripture says "there will be more joy in heaven over one sinner who repents than over ninety-nine just persons who need no repentance" (Lk 15:7). For our body is an image of the soul and the soul is an image of the Spirit. As the body without the soul is dead and cannot do anything, so without the heavenly soul—that is, without Holy Spirit—the soul is reckoned dead as far as the kingdom of God goes, being unable to do any of the things of God without the Holy Spirit. For as the Lord said "without Me you can do nothing" (Jn 15:5).

Prayer: My Lord, give me that holy birth from above, from Your heaven by Your Holy Spirit that I will be a true child of Yours, truly made in Your image. I am sorry for every time I drifted away from You. I never wish to betray You again, and to hear You saying, "I have nourished and brought up children, and they have rebelled against Me" (Is 1:2).

Look up at the greatest artist currently working on your portrait

4. The portrait painter needs to be attentive to the face of his subjects as he paints them. For the artist to excel in painting the portrait, he needs the face of the person to directly face him, face-to-face, in order to perfect his work. But if the subject turns his face away, then the painter is not able to paint because the face of the subject is not looking at him. In a similar way, the good portrait painter, Christ, requires those who believe in Him to gaze constantly towards Him so that He can paint His own image on them. Out of His Spirit, out of the substance of the light itself, the indescribable light, He paints a heavenly image "that He might present her to

Himself a glorious church, not having spot or wrinkle or any such thing, but that she should be holy and without blemish" (Eph 5:27). If anyone, therefore, does not continually gaze at Him, ignoring everything else, then the Lord will not paint His image with His own light. Therefore, it is necessary that we gaze continuously at Him, believing and loving Him, casting aside all worldly care and paying full attention to Him so that He may paint His own heavenly image on us and engrave it in our souls. Thus, putting on Christ, we may confidently receive the eternal life that begins here.

Are you a genuine or a fake coin?

5. A golden coin that does not receive the imprint of the king's image is not considered genuine and so will neither reach the marketplace nor be stored up in the royal treasuries, but will be discarded as fake. Similarly, if the soul does not have the image of the Holy Spirit stamped on it in indescribable light, it is not useful for the treasuries above and is cast out by the merchants of the kingdom, the apostles. In the same way, the man who was invited and yet did not wear a wedding garment was cast out as a stranger into the darkness for not wearing the heavenly image (Mt 22:11-13). The Spirit of the indescribable light is the mark and sign of the Lord stamped on souls. And as a dead body is useless and carried outside the city to be buried, so also the soul which does not bear the heavenly image of the divine light, which is the life of the soul, is rejected and completely cast out. For a dead soul is of no profit to the city of the saints, since it does not carry the radiance of the Holy Spirit. For just as the soul is the life of the body when it is in the world, so also the life of the soul is the Spirit of the Holy Trinity in the eternal and heavenly world.

6. Therefore, whoever seeks to be united to the Lord must plead with Him to send the Holy Spirit to him or her who is still living on Earth. For the Spirit is the life of the soul, and this is why the Lord came, to give His Spirit to every soul on Earth. The gospel illustrated this clearly:

"On the last day, that great day of the feast, Jesus stood and cried out, saying, 'If anyone thirsts, let him come to Me and drink. He who believes in Me, as the Scripture has said, out of his heart will flow rivers of living water.' But this He spoke concerning the Spirit, whom those believing in Him would receive; for the Holy Spirit was not yet given, because Jesus was not yet glorified" (Jn 7:37-39).

He also says "while you have the light, believe in the light... the night is coming when no one can work" (Jn 12:36, 9:4). Therefore, if anyone does not receive life for his or her soul (namely, the Holy Spirit) then that person will already head for the places of darkness when departing from his or her body. That person will not come into the Kingdom of Heaven, but will end in hell with "the devil and his angels" (Mt 25:41).

Gold and silver are items that become purer and more refined when thrown into the fire, but they then destroy all things that touch them, for they also become fire as they take on the nature of fire. Likewise, the souls that are plunged into the fire of the Holy Spirit will suffer no harm from any of the evil spirits. Even if evil powers try to come near them, the heavenly fire of the Spirit consumes them. A bird does not worry or fear the bird-catchers or the dangerous beasts when it flies up high. From its very high position, it laughs at everything below. So also, the soul that has received the wings of the Spirit flies up into the heights of heaven and then looks down on all the evil powers as it is higher than anything else.

Prayer: My Lord, imprint the image of Your Holy Spirit on me that I may become a genuine coin profitable for the work of Your kingdom and worthy to be added to Your treasure. Let Your Holy Spirit dwell in me to give me real life. I want to be united with You and am thirsty for Your beauty and hungry for Your presence. Give me wings to fly into Your presence and take Your gifts.

The dark day of humanity

7. In the day when Adam fell, God came walking into the garden. He wept, so to speak, at seeing Adam, one could imagine that He supposedly said; "After such good things, what evils you have chosen! After such glory, what shame you now bear! What darkness you are now in! What corruption! You fell from such light; what darkness has covered you!" When Adam fell, he became dead in the eyes of God, and the Creator wept over him. The angels, all the powers, the heavens, the earth and all creatures mourned his fall and death. For they saw the one who had been given to them as their king, becoming the servant of an opposing and evil power. Therefore, darkness became the garment of his soul, a bitter and evil darkness, for he was made a subject of the prince of darkness. He is the person who was wounded by robbers and left half dead as he was going down from Jerusalem to Jericho (Lk 10:30).

Adam, Lazarus, the traveller to Jericho and you

8. Lazarus, whom the Lord raised up, died and a rotten smell came from his dead body so that no one could approach his tomb. He is a symbol of Adam whose soul rotted with a great stench and was full of darkness. When you hear about Adam, Lazarus and the traveler

who the thieves wounded while he was on his journey from Jerusalem to Jericho (Lk 10:30-37), do not consider them as historical characters or distant stories, but think of yourself as you also carry the same darkness, the same smell and the same wounds.

We are all Adam's children of that dark race and we all inherit the same stench. Therefore, we all also suffer the torment that he suffered. For this suffering has battered us, as Isaiah says,

> "from the sole of the foot even to the head, there is no soundness in it, but wounds and bruises and putrefying sores; they have not been closed or bound up, or soothed with ointment" (Is 1:6).

Thus, we were wounded with an incurable wound. Only the Lord could heal us all. For this, He came personally because none of the patriarchs or the Law itself or the prophets were able to heal us. He alone, when He came, healed that sore, the incurable sore of the soul.

He is our food, drink and eternal life
9. Let us, therefore, receive God the Lord, the true healer, who alone can come to heal our souls, after He endured so much on our behalf. For He is always knocking at the doors of our hearts in order that we may open up to Him so that He may enter in and take His rest in our souls, and that we may wash His feet and He may come and dwell with us, as He promised "Behold, I stand at the door and knock. If anyone hears My voice and opens the door, I will come in to him and dine with him, and he with Me" (Rev 3:20). He endured much suffering by giving His body over to death and redeeming us from slavery in order to come to our souls and dwell in us. For this reason, the Lord says to those on his left side at the

time of judgment, "I was hungry and you gave Me no food; I was thirsty and you gave Me no drink; I was a stranger and you did not take Me in" (Mt 25:42-43). For His food and drink and clothing and shelter and rest are in our souls. Therefore, whenever He comes to us knocking, seeking to enter us, let us receive Him and lead Him into ourselves, because only He Himself is our food, drink and eternal life. Sadly now, every person who has not received Him inside himself or herself and has not found rest in Him, does not have an inheritance in the Kingdom of Heaven nor can he or she enter the heavenly city.

Our Lord Jesus Christ, lead us into the kingdom of heaven, as we glorify Your name with the Father and the Holy Spirit forever. Amen.

Chapter 21

Glorious Resurrection

Homily 21: Christians' glory dwells now in their souls, and will be shown openly at the time of the resurrection in their glorified bodies, in proportion to their piety.

The Holy Spirit wraps the resurrected bodies with glory

1-3. There are many different languages in the world, for each nation has its own language. But Christians have just one language as they are all taught one wisdom from God, a wisdom which is not from the world. Saint James contrasts the wisdom that is from above with the wisdom of this world when he says

"Who is wise and understanding among you? Let him show by good conduct that his works are done in the meekness of wisdom. But if you have bitter envy and self-seeking in your hearts, do not boast and lie against the truth. This wisdom does not descend from above, but is earthly, sensual, demonic. For where envy and self-seeking exist, confusion and every evil thing are there. But the wisdom that is from above is first pure, then peaceable, gentle, willing to yield, full of mercy and good fruits, without partiality and without hypocrisy" (Jm 3:13-17).

Christians discover a newer, deeper and heavenly understanding of the mysteries of God by observing all that God has created in this world. They see that God has created many different types of animals that have different habitats and characteristics. There are also many different varieties of plants, seeds, fish, birds and everything else that God created. Though each species is different from all the others, individuals within each species share the same characteristics. So also, the saints have their roots in one heaven and in one God, the Father, Son and Holy Spirit. They have different personalities and characters but share the same mind and heart as Saint Paul said,

"there are diversities of gifts, but the same Spirit. There are differences of ministries, but the same Lord. And there are diversities of activities, but it is the same God who works all in all. But the manifestation of the Spirit is given to each one for the profit of all...but one and the same Spirit works all these things, distributing to each one individually as He wills" (1 Cor 12:4-7,11).

Take the example of seeds that have inside them the characteristics which determine the size, shape, color, smell and use of the plants that grow from them. So also, those Christians who are deemed worthy to possess heavenly white clothing while on earth, have the glory of God hidden in their souls. At the time of the final resurrection, after all creation ceases to exist, the heavenly white robe that they had within their souls while they were on the earth, will adorn their naked bodies as they rise from their tombs in glory. Because they took hold of the kingdom of heaven and tasted heavenly nourishment by living with the Holy Spirit, that same Spirit will cover and warm them completely at the time of the final resurrection.

Prayer: My dear Lord, I have been born in You in baptism, buried with You, shared Your body and blood in Holy Communion and carried Your image in me. Please change me completely from inside and fill me with Your glorious light that will be my robe, my cover and my glory at the time of Your coming.

The heavens and the shadow of the heavens

4,5. In the Old Testament, God instructed His people saying "among the animals, whatever divides the hoof, having cloven hooves and chewing the cud—that you may eat" (Lev 11:2-3). You may wonder about the significance of the animals that have a divided hoof. This symbolizes those who walk upright in the Law, as they like these animals, travel securely along the road. The Law of Moses is a shadow of the new covenant. But as the shadow of a person is unable to perform any physical actions (for a shadow cannot bind up wounds or give food or speak), neither is the law able to accomplish the work of the new covenant. The shadow of the body comes from the body, exists because of the body, and can be seen before the body. It indicates that the body is present. But a shadow cannot bind up wounds, speak or give food. The Old Testament is the shadow of the new covenant that demonstrates the truth in advance, but cannot accomplish the work of the Spirit (2 Cor 3:8). The law of Moses, having been clothed in flesh, was unable to enter into peoples' hearts and take away the disgusting garments of darkness. But only the spiritual power of the

Holy Spirit and heavenly fire proceeding from the Fire of God can dissolve the power of darkness and evil. Circumcision, in the shadow of the Law, was a sign of the true circumcision of the heart, which came afterwards. The baptism of the Law was a shadow of the true things to come. For that baptism washed the body, but now the baptism of fire from the Holy Spirit purifies and cleanses polluted minds as John the Baptist said, "I indeed baptized you with water, but He will baptize you with the Holy Spirit" (Mk 1:8).

There the priest "since he himself is also subject to weakness" (Heb 5:2), entered into the Holy of Holies to offer sacrifices for himself and for the people. But, here the true High Priest, Christ, once and for all entered the heavenly altar (in the tabernacle which was not made by hands) in order to purify those who come to Him, for He says "I am with you always, even to the end of the age" (Mt 28:20). The high priest had on his chest two precious stones that had on them the names of the twelve patriarchs. This was done figuratively in that time, as a symbol of the Lord Jesus Christ, our true High Priest, who put on His Twelve Apostles and sent them as evangelists and preachers to the whole world. You can see how the shadow precedes the truth and shows it to us. But, as shadows are not able to perform any actions, nor ease suffering, so also the ancient Law of Moses was unable to heal the wounds and ease the suffering of souls, for it did not possess life.

> "So let no one judge you in food or in drink, or regarding a festival or a new moon or Sabbaths, which are a shadow of things to come, but the substance is of Christ... therefore, if you died with Christ from the basic principles of the world, why, as though living in the world, do you

subject yourselves to regulations— 'Do not touch, do not taste, do not handle,' which all concern things which perish with the using—according to the commandments and doctrines of men? These things indeed have an appearance of wisdom in self-imposed religion, false humility, and neglect of the body, but are of no value against the indulgence of the flesh" (Col 2:16-23).

We should feel very sorry for every soul that does not have the fellowship of the Holy Spirit

6. There are many examples of two elements joined together to create one perfect thing. The holy scripture has been given to us in two covenants. Humans were made according to the image of God and have two eyes, two eyebrows, two hands and two feet. It is regrettable if a person loses one eye or one hand or one foot. If a bird, for example, has only one wing, it is unable to fly with it. So also, a person who remains all alone and does not become united in fellowship with God's heavenly nature (that is, with the Holy Spirit) is not complete. And, this person remains "wretched, miserable, poor, blind, and naked" (Rev 3:17) and is not cleansed from immorality. For the soul itself has been called the temple of God and His dwelling place and also the bride of the King. For the Bible says "I will dwell in them and walk among them. I will be their God, and they shall be My people" (2 Cor 6:16). So God was pleased to come down from the holy heavens and take on Himself your physical nature. He took flesh from the earth and joined it with His Divine Spirit, so that you, who are from the earth, might receive a heavenly soul. When your soul has fellowship with the Holy Spirit, and His heavenly soul enters your soul, you are a perfect person in God, and an heir and son of God.

7. Neither all the ages of the heavens above nor all the ages of the earth below can grasp the greatness of God, as He is incomprehensible. Nor can the worlds above nor the worlds on earth understand the humility of God and how He could become little and simple to those who are humble and small. Both His smallness and His lowliness are just as incomprehensible as His greatness. For

> "Jesus, knowing that the Father had given all things into His hands, and that He had come from God and was going to God, rose from supper and laid aside His garments, took a towel and girded Himself. After that, He poured water into a basin and began to wash the disciples' feet, and to wipe them with the towel with which He was girded" (Jn 13:3-5).

Double honor instead of shame

7, 8. If you feel that God has allowed troubles and humiliations to come to you, know that one day you will discover that the things you thought were against you were the very things that gave your soul a great advantage. Perhaps, one day you wished to gain honor, richness or a good position in this world and instead you faced every kind of misfortune and difficulty. Only when you reason with yourself, accept the cross, renounce the world and return fully to God in humility, then you will begin to give thanks to God for the misfortune you had, like Saint Paul who was "not disobedient to the heavenly vision" (Acts 26:19). So, if you decide to change your mind and forsake the world and its desires, then, this means you have renounced worldly wisdom and accepted heavenly wisdom. After this, you will fully understand that you can only obtain true rest and happiness when you live with the Lord and are fully united with Him. Consequently, you will know that you have become free from the world and its ties, as our Lord said "if the Son makes you free, you shall be free indeed" (Jn 8:36).

When you think that you have made all the effort by renouncing the things which tie you to the world, then the Lord will call you to account, saying, "what do you boast in? Did I not give you your body and soul? What did you do?" If your soul begins to confess to the Lord and say "all things belong to You. The house I am in is Yours. My job is a gift from you. My clothing is Yours. I am nourished by You and You provide me with everything I need", then the Lord will answer you saying; "I thank you for saying this. Those possessions are now all yours. The good will you have is yours. Because of your love towards Me and because you have taken your refuge in Me, come to Me and I will give you all the things you did not possess until now, which no one possesses on earth. Receive Me, your Lord, into your soul that you may always be with Me in joy and happiness."

Prayer: My Lord, in the old times You showed me the shadow of Your way of salvation, but afterwards, You came in a body exactly like mine to show me the truth of Your love. Please unite Your Spirit with my soul so that I live through Your life-giving Spirit. From now on, I know that all the troubles in my way are there to give me glory at Your second coming. Help me to renew my mind to renounce all worldly honor and richness to find my real happiness and total rest in You.

Give it all despite suffering, to have it all under the tutorship of the Holy Spirit

9,10. Take the example of a woman who is engaged to a man. She brings all her possessions and jewelry out of her great love and casts them into his hands, saying "I consider nothing my own. All that I possess is yours. My treasures, my soul, my heart and my body are all yours." In the same way, the wise soul, as the bride of the Lord, has communion with the Holy Spirit. For when you decide to free yourself from the habits of the world to start seeking God, then you enter into a battle with your old nature which desires to keep its old habits and the customs which you grew up with.

You start waging a war against your own old thoughts as they try to drag you down and keep you occupied with the material world, which you intend to forsake. As you begin to fight the war between your desire to follow God and your old nature, you pit thoughts against thoughts, mind against mind, soul against soul, spirit against spirit, and your soul experiences agony. But it is necessary that you suffer with Him just as He suffered and was crucified for you, as "indeed we suffer with Him, that we may also be glorified together" (Rom 8:17). The Lord who is near to your soul and your body sees your battle and gives you power and puts heavenly thoughts inside you as He begins to give you rest internally. But He also allows grace to discipline and guide you. And when you reach this state of rest and surrender, grace makes you understand the path of your training and its advantages for your soul. It is like a rich man who sends his child to a tutor. For a while the tutor disciplines him in a way that seems harsh, until the child becomes an adult. Then he begins to be grateful to his tutor. God, also, in His prudence and love, chooses grace to discipline you until you become fully mature.

He is calling us all for salvation

11. The farmer scatters seed everywhere, in all directions. And the vinedresser (Jn 15:1) looks for fruit

on all the branches of the vine. So he will be really sad if he finds no fruit. Similarly, the Lord wishes His word to be sown in the hearts of all people everywhere. But just as the farmer is saddened by the unfertile earth, so the Lord is grieved with the barren heart, which produces no fruit (2 Cor 9:10). Just as the wind blows everywhere over all creation, and as the sun illuminates the whole universe, so God the Trinity exists everywhere and can be found everywhere. If you seek Him in the heavens (Ps 139:8), there He is found in the thoughts of angels. If you seek Him on earth, here also He is found in the hearts of people. But only a few out of these many people are Christians, those who are found to be pleasing to Him.

    Glory and majesty to the Father and Son and Holy Spirit forever. Amen

Chapter 22

The True Christians

Homily 38: We need accurate and correct understanding in order to discern who are true Christians.

Real or Fake?
1. Some people are considered Christians by others merely because they have the outward appearance of righteousness. But, only those who bear the sign and image of the King, Jesus Christ, are true Christians. The rest are fake Christians and bogus workers who imitate the work of real Christians. Saint Paul explained to us that "for he is not a Jew who is one outwardly, nor is circumcision that which is outward in the flesh, but he is a Jew who is one inwardly, and circumcision is that of the heart, in the spirit, not in the letter; whose praise is not from men but from God" (Rom 2:28-29). True Christians and fake ones can look very similar in their external appearance and behavior, to the extent that they could deceive many people. Only experienced spiritual people can differentiate between the two. Fake Christians can even look like apostles who

appear to suffer for the sake of Christ and for preaching about the kingdom of heaven. For this reason, the apostle said he was "in labors more abundant, in stripes above measure, in prisons more frequently" (2 Cor 11:23). Saint Paul warned us about those people, saying "for such are false apostles, deceitful workers, transforming themselves into apostles of Christ" (2 Cor 11:13). Also, Saint John advised us about them saying, "eloved, do not believe every spirit, but test the spirits, whether they are of God; because many false prophets have gone out into the world" (1 Jn 4:1).

Prayer: My dear Lord, please help me to become a real Christian, a real child of Yours inwardly, not minding how I look to other people outwardly. Make me a real worker in Your ministry; cleanse me from any deceitful intentions or desires which do not give glory to Your name. I do not want to hear Your voice saying "I never knew you, depart from me." Please put Your image on me and help me to resemble You. I have no experience to help me to know what is good for me but I rely completely on You to rescue me from the devil and his workers.

Remove that veil from your heart

2,3. The genuine pearls and precious stones that are fit for the king's crown are unique and rare. So also, real Christians are shaped and crafted into the crown of Christ so that they may have fellowship with the saints. Glory to God, who loved people so much, and suffered on their behalf and raised them from the dead.

You need to be vigilant so that there is no veil covering your heart to prevent you from looking at the glory of God, like the Israelites who could not look at Moses' face because of the veil (Exod 34:33-35) which still remains on some hearts (2 Cor 3:13-15). Surely, when the veil is taken away, Christ appears and shows

Himself to those who are true Christians, who truly love Him and seek Him in truth. He says "I will manifest myself to him" (Jn 14:21) and "we will come to him and make Our home with him" (Jn 14:23). When the veils are removed away from our hearts, then we can clearly see the Lord and say "we all, with unveiled face beholding as in a mirror the glory of the Lord, are being transformed into the same image from glory to glory, just as by the Spirit of the Lord" (2 Cor 3:18). Therefore, let us work hard to come to Christ who never lies, to receive His promise, which is the new covenant, which the Lord made through His cross when he crushed the gates of hell and sin. He retrieved the faithful souls and gave them the Holy Spirit to live inside them (the Comforter) and brought them back to His kingdom. Let us reign with Him in his city Jerusalem, the heavenly church, in the gathering of the saintly angels.

Prayer: My dear Lord, please take away from me the veil of arrogance, lust, sin, fear, and the love of the world, so that I can clearly see You in my life. Please shape me to be a genuine pearl or a precious stone so that I become fit to be with all the saints in the clouds with You. Help me to hold on to my crown so that no one can take it from me. Work with me as You promised to change me into Your image so that I will be with You in the new Jerusalem that comes down from heaven.

Hold fast what you have, that no one may take your crown

4. Some people have developed self-confidence, thinking that the grace of God has fully sanctified them, believing that they cannot contain any lust. As their minds have reached heavenly and divine matters, they think they have already attained perfection. But when someone supposes that he has reached a calm harbor,

then strong waves rise against him, and he finds himself in the midst of the ocean where death is all around. In this way, pride has allowed sin to enter and it produced all manner of evil desire (Rom 7:8). One may wonder why this change keeps occurring. It is Satan who hates all goodness and suggests evil things to those who are pursuing virtue. He tries to wrestle them down to the ground; this is his work. This is why Saint Peter advised us to "be sober, be vigilant; because your adversary the devil walks about like a roaring lion, seeking whom he may devour" (1 Pet 5:8).

In contrast, there are some other people who have received some grace from God, like a drop from the depths of a great sea, which grows in them hour by hour and day by day. Though they feel the effect of God's work in them, they cannot comprehend how or why they were found worthy to receive this grace and enlightenment. Gradually, the grace of the Holy Spirit enlightens them, guides them and turns them towards good in every way. As they know that this grace is heavenly and divine, they recognize that they are more royal than many kings, governors and nobles for the Spirit says about the Son that He "loved us and washed us from our sins in His own blood, and has made us kings and priests to His God and Father" (Rev 1:5-6). But after a little while, as they fully comprehend the love and mercy of God, each of those who is truly enlightened by the Holy Spirit considers himself or herself to be the chief sinner.

Trust in the Lord who guides you

While you work to accomplish inward righteousness, don't ever submit yourselves to Satan, but "submit to God. Resist the devil, and he will flee from you" (Jm 4:7). This way, the testimony of your conscience may find glory in the cross of Christ. The blood of sacrificial animals in the old covenant purified people externally, so

> "how much more shall the blood of Christ, who through the eternal Spirit offered Himself without spot to God, cleanse your conscience from dead works to serve the living God?" (Heb 9:14)

Then you may say "we know what we worship" (Jn 4:22). Trust in God who guides you and obey Him. Let your soul remain in fellowship with God as the bride joins to the bridegroom, for 'this is a great mystery, but I speak concerning Christ" and the spotless soul (Eph 5:32).

Glory to Him forever. Amen.

Chapter 23

The Purpose of Divine Scripture
Homily 39

Take the example of a king who writes letters to those he wishes to give special privileges to. He writes to all of them saying "hurry at once to come to me and receive royal gifts from me." But, if they do not come and receive them, they will gain nothing just for having read the letters. Rather, they are in danger of punishment for having refused to come and to accept the honor the king wishes to give them. So also, God, the true King, has sent His divine scriptures to people as letters, pointing out to them that they need to call out to God, and then, believing, they need to ask and to receive a heavenly gift from God the Holy Trinity Himself. For it is written "that through these you may be partakers of the divine nature" (2 Pet 1:4). But if a person does not approach and seek and receive, it will not benefit him or her to read the scriptures. But rather he or she is under the sentence of death, because he or she did not wish to receive the gift of life from the heavenly King, without which it is impossible to obtain immortal life, which is Christ. "For everyone who asks receives, and he who seeks finds, and to him who knocks it will be opened" (Lk 11:10).

Glory to God forever. Amen.

Chapter 24

Put Off the Old Man

Homily 42: Not external things, but interior things can come against or hurt a person, namely, the Spirit of grace or the spirit of evil.

You will be toiled and sawn at times of troubles
     1,2. A city that once was great but is now razed to nothing by her enemies, as there were no strong walls to protect her, has no current value. In like manner, souls adorned with knowledge, intelligence, charm and sharp minds are like great cities that must be fortified by the power of the Holy Spirit, so that the enemies may not enter and lay them desolate. For the wise men and philosophers of this world such as Aristotle, Plato or Socrates were like great cities as they were skilled in knowledge with great intelligence, but were laid waste by the enemies because the Spirit of God was not in them. However, many simple people who receive grace

are like little cities fortified by the power of Christ. They only fall away from grace for two reasons; 1) either because they do not persevere patiently in bearing the afflictions brought to them, or 2) because they have tasted the pleasures of sin and continued in them.

Those who journey towards God cannot reach their goal without many trials. When giving birth, a beggar and a queen both have the same sufferings, so likewise neither the land of a rich man nor the land of a poor man can produce worthy fruit unless the land is toiled. So too in the working of the soul, neither the wise man nor the rich man grows in grace, unless it is through patience and many labors. Every time you face trouble remember that the Spirit says "for indeed I am for you, and I will turn to you, and you shall be tilled and sown" (Ezk 36:9).

Do good to all as your Lord does

For the life of Christians ought to be like sweet honey without any bitterness. Such Christians should be good to all who approach them, whether good or bad, as the Lord say; "you shall be perfect, just as your Father in heaven is perfect" (Mt 5:48). For what injures and corrupts a person is from within "for out of the heart proceed evil thoughts, murders, adulteries, fornications, thefts, false witness, blasphemies" (Mt 15:19).

Be very attentive to get rid of the old man

3. It is "the old man" (2 Cor 5:17) who is the source of evil within the soul that works as a veil of darkness. But those who seek God must put off "the old man which grows corrupt according to the deceitful lusts" (Eph 4:22) and must put on the heavenly new man that is Christ. After this they can say all things have become new (2 Cor 5:17). Thus, nothing of the things

outside people can harm them except the spirit of darkness that remains alive and active in their hearts. So therefore, each person in his or her thoughts must reject the suggestions of evil in order for Christ to shine in his or her heart.

Prayer: My Lord, I know that there is still darkness deep within me, inside my soul. Please work with me to take away my old nature, the old man, and to put on Christ by being one with You, united with Your Holy Spirit who is more than capable of moving me from under the power of darkness into the freedom of the children of God. Otherwise, I will be like a city with no walls or like unploughed land that never produces any good fruit. Please dwell deep inside me and work in me continuously so that I am truly formed in Your image.

Glory to Him forever. Amen.

Chapter 25

The Indwelling of the Spirit

Homily 49: Rejecting all the pleasures of this world without obtaining the full grace of the Holy Spirit is a double loss.

The joy of the Holy Spirit instead of the joy of the world
  1,2. If anyone renounces all the pleasures of this world for the sake of the Lord but still does not find the joy of the Holy Spirit instead of the joy of the world, he or she endures a double loss as he or she cuts off the relationship to the world but does not gain the reward of the fellowship of the Holy Spirit. If he or she does not know with confidence the satisfying communion with the heavenly Bridegroom in his or her soul, instead of the temporal and sensual communion with this world, he or she has not yet been clothed with the clothing of the light of the Holy Trinity, instead of the perishable clothing of this world of darkness. This one is pitiful above all. This one has been deprived of the passing pleasures of this world, yet has not enjoyed the divine gifts of the Holy Spirit. It is in order to experience the divine mysteries of

the Holy Spirit in the inner soul, that a person becomes a stranger to the world so that his or her soul may pass on to eternity as the apostle says "our citizenship is in heaven" (Phil 3:20), and also "for though we walk in the flesh, we do not war according to the flesh" (2 Cor 10:3).

Therefore, it is necessary that people who cast off the things of this world must believe deeply in themselves that they must now mentally pass from this world into the coming age, through the Holy Spirit. Only this way can they continue to experience full pleasure and enjoyment in their spiritual relationships with the Holy Spirit, as their inner 'man' (soul) is born again of the Spirit. The Lord said "he who hears My word and believes in Him who sent Me has everlasting life, and shall not come into judgment, but has passed from death into life" (Jn 5:24). Indeed, there is another death other than the physical one and another life other than the visible one. For scripture says "she who lives in pleasure is dead while she lives" (1 Tim 5:6) and "let the dead bury their own dead, but you go and preach the kingdom of God" (Lk 9:60). Moreover, the Spirit says "blessed and holy is he who has part in the first resurrection. Over such the second death has no power, but they shall be priests of God and of Christ, and shall reign with Him a thousand years" (Rev 20:6).

Returning to our heavenly home

3. For as the sun spreads its rays wholly on the earth when it rises, but withdraws all of its light once again when it sets, so too the soul that is not reborn from above of the Spirit is totally scattered, in thoughts and mind, over the earth. But, when it is deemed worthy to receive the heavenly birth and communion of the Holy Spirit, it takes all its thoughts and emotions back to the Lord into the heavenly dwelling that is not made by

hands. In doing so, all of its being becomes heavenly, pure and holy, passing into the divine realm. For the soul, rescued from the dark prison of the wicked ruler of this world, finds pure and divine thoughts in God, because it pleased God to give people "exceedingly great and precious promises, that through these you may be partakers of the divine nature, having escaped the corruption that is in the world through lust" (2 Pet 1:4).

Prayer: My Lord, give me the will to bring all my thoughts, motives and emotions back to You, and to genuinely make myself a stranger to all the pleasure and false glory of this world, and even to all people, that I may find the true joy of Your Holy Spirit in me. Then, I will fully understand Your love and the pleasure of being Your child. Make me experience your resurrection by being born again in You by Your Holy Spirit, so that I will be freed from the prison of darkness and overcome the second death by Your divine power.

You are the house of God and His treasure

4. When you persevere in prayers and reject all worldly pleasures, you will find rest and joy as you clearly see God dwelling in your body. Oh, the love of God that He should give Himself as a gift to those who believe that in their time on earth, they will possess God and God will dwell in them. For as God created the sky and the earth as a dwelling place for humans, He created human bodies and souls as dwelling places fit for Himself to abide in. The Lord wishes to have humans, who are created in His image, as beautiful dwelling places, and as a beautiful bride. For the apostle says "I have betrothed you to one husband, that I may present you as a chaste virgin to Christ" (2 Cor 11:2). And again, "Christ as a Son over His own house, whose house we are if we hold fast the confidence and the rejoicing of the hope firm to the

end" (Heb 3:6). And, just as we all try to store in our houses all good things, so also the Lord stores up in His house (our souls and our bodies) all the heavenly treasures of the Spirit.

Listen: This is God; the soul is not God. This is Lord; that is servant. This is Creator; that is creature. This is Maker; that is the thing that is made. There is nothing common to God's nature that is also common to the human soul. But by means of His incomprehensible love, it pleased Him to make His dwelling in this created thing, this intellectual creature, this precious and extraordinary work; "that we might be a kind of first fruits of His creatures" (Jm 1:18).

5. Therefore, since such good things are offered to us and such amazing promises have been given, let us not neglect nor delay our progress towards eternal life and let us give ourselves up completely to the love of the Lord. Let us then call out to the Lord so that, by His own power, He may redeem us from the prison of the darkness of shameful desires and He may make His own image shine splendidly in our souls. And thus, we may be deemed worthy of the fellowship of the Holy Spirit, as we glorify the Father and the Son and the Holy Spirit forever. Amen.

Chapter 26

The Treasure of the Spirit in Clay Vessels

Homily 50: God is the one who works wonders through His saints.

God works in His saints
1,2,3. I wonder whether it was Elijah or God in him who commanded the rain not to fall on earth? I believe that He who holds the power over heaven and earth was seated Himself in the mind of Elijah and through his tongue the Word of God forbade the rain from falling on the earth (1 Kings 17:1-7). When He spoke again, the gates of heaven opened and rain poured down (1 Kings 18:41-45). In the same manner, David, without any weapon, was able to fight against a famous giant and killed him with a sling and a stone. It was the divine nature itself that killed him and brought about the victory. For David could not have done it, as he was weak in his body. Likewise, also Moses laid down a rod and it became a serpent (Exod 7:10). He spoke and it became a rod. When he struck the rod, there came forth lice and

frogs (Exod 8:6,17). When he spoke to the sea, it was divided (Exod 14:16, 21), and when he spoke to the river, it was changed into blood. It is evident that a heavenly power was dwelling in his mind and through it Moses did all these signs as his own nature could not do these things. Therefore, when the Lord told him to depart and go up to a land flowing with milk and honey, Moses answered, "if your presence does not go with us, do not bring us up from here" (Exod 33:15). Then, when Joshua came to Jericho, and besieged it for seven days, he was unable to do anything out of his own nature, but then God commanded the walls and they came tumbling down by themselves. And who is it who commanded the sun to stand still for another two hours in the conflict of war (Josh 10:13)? Was it Joshua's own nature or the power that stood by him? It was indeed by the power of God who dwelt in all of them that those miracles happened with such ease. Let me tell you that although those things truly took place, they were symbols and shadows of true realities. For when you raise your heart and mind towards Heaven, clinging to the Lord, Satan will be weakened by the power of God that dwells in you. So, as the walls of Jericho fell by God's power, so also the walls of evil that obstruct your mind and your heart now will be totally destroyed by God's power.

The coming of Christ and the fullness of the Holy Spirit

4. If the Holy Spirit was poured out with such mysterious force on things that were only a shadow of the things to come, the outpouring of the Spirit takes place with much more power in the new covenant, due to the utmost richness of the mercy of God. For the Bible says "it shall come to pass in the last days, says God, that I will pour out of My Spirit on all flesh" (Acts 2:17). This is what the Lord himself said "I am with you

always, even to the end of the age" (Mt 28:20). "For everyone who asks receives, and he who seeks finds, and to him who knocks it will be opened" (Mt 7:8). He also says "If you then, being evil, know how to give good gifts to your children, how much more will your heavenly Father give the Holy Spirit to those who ask Him!" (Lk 11:13). Our message comes "in power, and in the Holy Spirit and in much assurance" as the apostle says (1 Thess 1:5). All these wonderful spiritual gifts are found after much pain, work, patience and love for God as the senses of the soul are being trained by the Holy Spirit through good and evil as it is written "solid food belongs to those who are of full age, that is, those who by reason of use have their senses exercised to discern both good and evil" (Heb 5:14).

The Holy Spirit is your helper to the end of your life

If a person knows the deceitful power of evil that desires to defile the soul of every person and does not fully receive the help of the Holy Spirit that strengthens our weakness and renews our soul with joy, he or she travels in the world without the endless provision of God's grace and His continuous fatherly care. On the other hand, when a person is helped by the Lord and finds spiritual happiness and heavenly gifts, then he or she would be absolutely wrong to think that sin can no longer shackle him or her. This person would be oblivious to the trickery of the devil who murdered many souls from the beginning, if he or she thought like that. For this reason, the Lord said about the devil that "he was a murderer from the beginning, and does not stand in the truth, because there is no truth in him" (Jn 8:44). You must understand that people grow in the grace of God from infancy to perfection in Christ. For this reason, Saint Paul told the Corinthians "I, brethren, could not speak to you as spiritual people but as to carnal, to babes in Christ" (1 Cor 3:1). It is indeed through the work of the Holy Spirit that our faith increases and every stronghold of evil thoughts inside us is gradually destroyed, as the Bible says, "the weapons of our warfare are not carnal but mighty in God for pulling down strongholds" (2 Cor 10:4).

Ask yourself whether you have truly found Him

Therefore, each one of us must examine ourselves to determine whether or not we have found the treasure in earthen vessels (2 Cor 4:7), and whether we have put on the royal robe of the Holy Spirit, seen the King of Kings and found rest by becoming closer to Him. If not, perhaps we still serve in the most exterior parts of the house.

We have much more still to clarify together and call to your attention according to your disposition and sincerity, but we have briefly pointed out a beginning, so that, as people of understanding, you might work and examine the power of the words given to you and become more knowledgeable in the Lord, and increase in the simplicity of your heart through His grace and in the power of the truth, so that you may be found safe in your salvation with all assurance and may be freed from all the deceit of the adversary. Thus, you will receive the privilege of being found upright and without condemnation in the day of judgment of our Lord Jesus; to Him be glory forever. Amen.

Conclusion

Saint Macarius, through his deep understanding of the spiritual journey with God and towards God, used many illustrations and examples. We will endeavor to assimilate them according to their themes, in an attempt to consolidate our learning.

The value of the human soul
Saint Macarius opens our minds to very important concepts that make us understand how our loving God values each one of us. It is as if there are no other souls or creatures in the whole world apart from me (who is nothing in reality, unless God makes me everything He foresaw me to be). This understanding is an essential remedy for depression, especially as Beck (who is the founder of Cognitive Behavioral Therapy, CBT) described the psychological build-up of depression as a state of mood that occurs when you believe that; "life is pointless, future is hopeless and self is worthless". Saint Macarius shows us that the point of our existence in this life is that we should be filled with the light of the Holy Spirit regardless of any disappointments that we

might face or endure. Our future is to be in His kingdom with Him and to be like Him. Our souls are extremely valuable in the eyes of God

> "who loved us and washed us from our sins in His own blood, and has made us kings and priests to His God and Father, to Him be glory and dominion forever and ever" (Revelation 1:5-6).

This is based on the belief that man is made in the image of God (Homily 12). As man was created in the image of God

> "Adam was like a very valuable coin, made from pure gold, with the image of the sovereign King engraved on it. But, when he fell, the image of the King faded away and the nature of the coin changed into a cheap, fake metal. So, the coin lost its value and became good for nothing. That is what happened to Adam when he entertained evil intentions and accepted bad thoughts. He then lost God. Though Adam remained a living being (1 Cor 15:45), he was dead to God who looks into the minds and hearts of His creation. As good Christians turn their eyes away from evil scenes, God turns his eyes away from those who do evil" (Homily 12).

But Saint Macarius brings us to the living hope that is in Christ (1 Pet 1:3) as he explains how our "new nature that is united with God is far more honorable and glorified than Adam's first nature" because of our unity with the Lord Jesus Christ (Homily 16). So we can stop mourning the events that happened to Adam and start experiencing our new nature in Christ, who

> "abolished in His flesh the enmity, that is, the law of commandments contained in ordinances, so as

to create in Himself one new man from the two" (Ephesians 2:15).

Equally, we should move forward with Christ, letting go of painful childhood experiences, imperfect upbringing, neglect, unfavorable treatment, unfairly harsh criticism, regrettable mistakes, unfortunate events and hidden sins. This way, we can all go forward in our lives, no longer mourning our old nature, wishing it had been different from the one we have known, but celebrating the unity with Christ that makes us new people in Him according to His image and in accordance with His mercy.

Having established the new nature, Saint Macarius goes further to assert that,

> "Christians are not of this world; they are children of the heavenly Adam, a new race, children of the Holy Spirit, shining brothers of Christ, similar to their Father, the spiritual Adam" (Homily 16).

He strongly encourages us to acknowledge and enjoy our new nature in God,

> "Beloved, you must know that your intellectual soul has been given very much honor and dignity, and is considered by God to be very lovely and worthy. He takes pleasure in choosing your soul as His dwelling place, instead of the whole heavens and earth. Therefore, your immortal soul is like a precious vessel for the Holy Spirit" (Homily 26).

Therefore, he believes that,

> "God has called you to adoption and immortality as He said 'let Us make man in Our image, according to Our likeness' (Gen 1:26). Heaven and

earth will pass away, but you have been called to immortality, to be a son, a brother and a spouse of the King [...] you should now understand how precious you are in God's eyes and comprehend your dignity with which God has crowned you" (Homily 16).

Therefore, he adds,
"Great and indescribable are the promises held out to true Christians. They are so great, indeed, that all the glory and beauty of heaven and earth cannot measure up to the beauty and riches of a single Christian soul" (Homily 4).

Interestingly, he believes that the knowledge of the true value of our souls in God's eyes makes us humble, like Jesus Christ, who humbled Himself to reach out to us,
"O people, know your nobility and dignity. You are the brothers and sisters of Christ (Mk 3:35), the friends of the King (Song 5:16) and the bride of the heavenly Bridegroom (Rev 22:17). For the person who knows the dignity of his or her soul is also able to know the power and the mysteries of the Holy Trinity. This knowledge will only make people humbler, for the light of God makes people see their fallen state and appreciate the work of God in them" (Homily 27).

The living throne of God that is full of eyes
Saint Macarius likens the value of our soul to the throne of God. He explains how Ezekiel revealed to us,
"the mystery of the soul that would receive the Lord and become a throne for His glory [...] there is no part of the soul that is not full of the spiritual

eyes of light. That is to say, there is no part of the soul that is covered with darkness, as it has become totally light and spirit" (Homily 1).

On the contrary, when we are in unity with the dark forces of evil, we lose our dignity, and become so full of darkness that we become all darkness as Saint Paul said "you were once darkness" (Eph 5:8). Therefore, Saint Macarius explains to us that,

"Since sin entered into human minds and hearts, human souls became unruly and only interested in the company of other rowdy spirits, which are the devil and his followers. But, when Jesus rides on those wild souls (see Homily 1), He gradually tames the soul, making it a dwelling place for the Holy Spirit" (Homily 23).

"Finally, when it becomes worthy to join with the Holy Spirit, then it becomes all light, all eyes, all spirit, all joy, all rest, all happiness, all love, all compassion, all righteousness and all goodness" (Homily 18).

Saint Paul described this when he explained "for you were once darkness, but now you are light in the Lord" (Eph 5:8). But the Lord said "I am the light of the world. He who follows Me shall not walk in the darkness, but have the light of life" (Jn 8:12). Then we become fully united with the Holy Spirit and experience the full joy of being in Him (Homily 50), with Him and completely guided by Him until we reach the gates of heaven.

Saint Macarius gives us another illustration of true Christians becoming genuine jewels in the royal crown of Christ. He adds, "the genuine pearls and precious stones that are fit for the king's crown are unique and rare. So also, real Christians are shaped and crafted into the crown of Christ so that they may have fellowship with the saints" (Homily 38).

Illustrations of the work of the Holy Spirit in us

The blessed Saint Macarius teaches us that the Holy Spirit always works in us to bring us to Christ as "newborn babes" (1 Pet 2:2). He likens the work of the Holy Spirit to the continuous work of bees that secretly and patiently fashion their honeycomb in the hive till the final product of sweet honey is ready to be brought out; "the Holy Spirit secretly establishes His love in our hearts, changing our bitterness to His sweetness and our roughness into His gentleness" (Homily 16). He even goes further and gives a marvelous illustration of the Holy Spirit being like an artist who works with us to make us a subject of amazing beauty in God's eyes,

"He is like a distinguished artist sculpturing a statue, who partly covers some of the features that he is sculpturing, until he has finished all his work, and only then he holds it up to shine in the light in front of many people. So the Lord, who is the true artisan, engraves His image on our hearts and secretly renews our souls until our souls leave our bodies. Then He reveals the real beauty of those souls that He has worked on in front of all His saints and angels" (Homily 16).

He also likens the work of the Holy Spirit in our souls to the work of salt that preserves and seasons food to prevent it from going bad. He believes that,

"the apostles passed on to people the heavenly salt of the Holy Spirit, which seasons them to take away any decay and keep them free from every source of rot."

Therefore, he adds,
"every soul that is not seasoned with the salt of the Holy Spirit grows corrupt and is filled with the stench of bad thoughts, so that God turns away His face from the awful stench of vain thoughts and dark emotions that dwell in such a soul" (Homily 1).

Let us die to the world and ask the Holy Spirit to continuously work in us as the salt that seasons food and as the bee that fashions its hive to form us in the image of God.

We also need the oil and the yeast of the Holy Spirit
Saint Macarius introduces an inspiring idea that we need something much more powerful than ourselves and completely external to us and very different from our own nature to give us sustenance in our journey towards God, in order to bring us into unity with Him. He clearly identifies the Holy Spirit as oil that is essential for us. Moreover, he links the oil of the Holy Spirit to the anointing of all the kings. He considers all of us, who are united with Christ, to be kings through the anointing of the Holy Spirit. He says,
"as we can see in the scriptures, the anointing with oil was very awesome (1 Sam 16:13). Likewise, now those spiritual people who [...] have been anointed with the heavenly oil" also become kings, queens and prophets through the grace of God (Homily 17).

But in Homily 4, he expands on this concept using the parable of the five wise virgins, who took extra oil with them for their lamps, and the five foolish virgins who went out without having enough oil. Obviously, he meant the oil of the Holy Spirit. We need something that does not come from our human nature, but is divine i.e. the Holy Spirit as in the case of the five wise virgins (Homily 4). He says,

> "when we fell into sin, we received inside ourselves something that was foreign to our nature, namely, the corruption of our desires through the disobedience of the first man. This corrupted nature can only be expelled by something that is also foreign to our nature, that is the Holy Spirit" (Homily 4).

In the same manner, he uses the parable of the hidden leaven to stress the belief that our salvation is not through what we have, but through what we are given from God as a result of His loving grace. He explains,

> "the whole of mankind is like unleavened dough. But the holy leaven belongs to another world; it is the divine nature of the Holy Spirit. If therefore, the heavenly leaven of the Spirit (that is from another land) does not enter our lowly human nature, we remain unleavened and are not freed from the unleavened state of evil. However, when the holy Spirit fills us, we become leavened and useful as we are freed from all evil desires" (Homily 24).

This is to say that we need something that we do not naturally have, namely the oil and the yeast of the Holy Spirit. Therefore, he believes that those who have possessed the oil of the Holy Spirit and had their nature changed by the yeast of the Holy Spirit, have been sealed by the Spirit as a guarantee. This is what the Bible teaches us, that God "also has sealed us and given us the Spirit in our hearts as a guarantee" (2 Cor 1:22).

> "In Him you also trusted, after you heard the word of truth, the gospel of your salvation; in whom also, having believed, you were sealed with the Holy Spirit of promise" (Eph 1:13).

Therefore, he says in Homily 12,
> "in the last day, God will know His people as they too will know Him [...] He will know them by His seal on them, as John saw in his revelation: 'we have sealed the servants of our God on their foreheads'" (Rev 7:3).

The Holy Spirit guides us in our journey
Saint Macarius believes that it is the Holy Spirit who works in us all the time to deliver us to God as holy people, as Saint Paul also explained,
> "He might present her to Himself a glorious church, not having spot or wrinkle or any such thing, but that she should be holy and without blemish" (Ephesians 5:27).

He teaches us that it is also the Holy Spirit who guides us in our journey towards God. He reassures us that,
> "those who have been given 'the right to become children of God' (John 1:12) and to be born again of the Holy Spirit, are led by Him through many different paths while the grace of God continues to work secretly in their hearts to give them spiritual joy" (Homily 18).

It is clear that it is God who works in us, guide us, supports us and sanctifies us as Saint Paul said, "it is God who works in you both to will and to do for His good pleasure" (Phil 2:13). Therefore, we should feel secure in our living hope that God will do all things to change us into His image and guide us and deliver us safely to heaven as long as we live in obedience and submission to His will.

Garments of light and garments of darkness

You must have wondered about our outfit in heaven and what it is made of, as surely heaven will not have any earthly material such as wool, cotton, or silk. Saint Macarius tells us many things about the heavenly clothes of righteousness (Homilies 1 and 2). He gives us a deep understanding of Saint Paul's phrase, "put on the Lord Jesus Christ, and make no provision for the flesh, to fulfil its lusts" (Rom 13:14). He contrasts the effect of sin with the life of righteousness. The effect of sin is like being clothed in a cloak of darkness which covers all the senses, intentions and thoughts, making us live in darkness and lose our real selves. The Holy Spirit clothes the believing soul in the robe of righteousness and in light. Even more, as the soul puts on Christ, the old body is replaced with the new nature of Christ and the old natural eyes are replaced with new divine eyes. It is the same with all the old human senses until the person becomes all light and is clothed in white in the manner of those souls who have overcome evil (Rev 7:9). Accordingly, Saint Macarius teaches us that if we depart from this world without obtaining for ourselves these clothes of light and righteousness, then we will stand in front of God naked, which will certainly bring shame to our souls.

"For as far as anyone, through faith and passion, has been deemed worthy to receive the Holy Spirit, to that same degree his or her body will also be glorified in that day. What the soul now stores up within shall then be revealed as a treasure and displayed externally in the heavenly body" (Homily 5).

Therefore, he pleads with us saying,
"If you are not clothed with the Holy Spirit, then you are naked. Therefore, cry out to the Lord asking him to clothe you with His heavenly robe which is His Holy Spirit, for He gives the Holy Spirit to those who ask Him" (Homily 20).

But he warns us not to try to use anything apart from the Holy Spirit Himself to cover our nakedness because false covers do not offer any sense of security. He uses Adam as an example:
"Though Adam made himself a cover from fig leaves, he continued to feel his shame because he knew of his disgrace, poverty and nakedness [...] Therefore, you ought not to make yourself a false cover from self-righteousness or vain thoughts but to ask Christ to cover you with the genuine garment of the true light of his indescribable glory" (Homily 20).

He also uses the example of a seed that carries within it all its genetic characteristics which determine how it interacts with the environment and only reveals what is inside when it has died in the ground to produce the new life that was always stored inside it. He says,
"Take the example of seeds that have inside them the characteristics which determine the size,

shape, color, smell and use of plants that grow from them. So also, those Christians who are deemed worthy to possess heavenly white clothing while on earth, have the glory of God hidden in their souls. At the time of the final resurrection, after all creation ceases to exist, the heavenly white robe that they had within their souls while they were on the earth, will adorn their naked bodies as they rise from their tombs in glory. Because they took hold of the kingdom of heaven and tasted heavenly nourishment by living with the Holy Spirit, that same Spirit will cover and warm them completely at the time of the final resurrection" (Homily 32).

The Holy Spirit also gives us power to fulfil all righteousness

The Holy Spirit not only guides us in our journey, but also gives us real power to fulfil all of God's commandments to live in the joy of His fellowship. This happens when we persevere in our quest for Him with honesty and eagerness, proven by continuous prayers, fasting, obedience to His word and unfailing service. When He dwells in us, He makes things we previously found difficult easy and enjoyable. Saint Macarius teaches us saying,

"When the Lord dwells in you, all that you used to force yourself to do reluctantly, you will willingly and easily do in love. When you become mindful of the Lord, waiting for Him with an abundance of love in the Holy Spirit, the Lord will see your constant desire and diligence and how you have tamed your heart to do all good things even against your own nature. Then He will show you compassion and free you from the deep seated and hidden sins which previously overpowered you [...] thus, afterwards, you will find it very easy to do all the commandments of the Lord without any difficulty or need to force yourself because it will be the Lord himself, dwelling in you, who fulfils His own commandments in you. Following this, you will produce the fruit of the Spirit in all purity" (Homily 19).

The Holy Spirit gives us wings in our journey to fly to heavenly places
While we persevere in our journey towards God, Saint Macarius tells us that the Holy Spirit takes us up to heaven from time to time to check out our inheritance. He says:

"Someone may desire to fly into divine places to enjoy the liberty of the Holy Spirit (2 Cor 3:18), but if he or she is not given wings, this is not possible. Let us pray to God that He may give us the; "wings like a dove" (Ps 55:6), of the Holy Spirit so we may fly to Him and find rest" (Homily 2).

He goes on to explain why God did not create us with wings:

"When God created Adam, He did not furnish him with material wings as birds have, but He prepared for him the wings of the Holy Spirit to give him a taste of heaven. He will give him these wings at the resurrection, to lift him and direct him wherever the Spirit wishes. The saints are now already deemed worthy to possess these wings to fly up in their minds to the realm of heavenly thoughts" (Homily 5).

As we receive the wings of the Holy Spirit we rise above all troubles and weakness. He expands saying,

> "A bird does not worry or fear the bird-catchers or the dangerous beasts when it flies up high. From its very high position, it laughs at everything below. So also, the soul that has received the wings of the Spirit flies up into the heights of heaven and then looks down on all the evil powers as it is higher than anything else" (Homily 30).

The book of Revelation gives us a very similar idea:

> "Now when the dragon saw that he had been cast to the earth, he persecuted the woman who gave birth to the male Child. But the woman was given two wings of a great eagle, that she might fly into the wilderness to her place, where she is nourished for a time and times and half a time, from the presence of the serpent" (Rev 12: 13-14).

New discerning eyes

Like heavenly birds, in addition to the wings, we need new spiritual eyes that can discern what is good from what is bad, and look out for the way of heaven. He says,

> "Those who strive to live a true Christian life must, above all, develop their soul's ability to understand and discern what is right [...] this ability to distinguish what is right becomes like an eye, so that we can escape all fellowship with evil and receive the divine gift of the Holy Spirit and so become worthy to be with the Lord [...] moreover, if he is not diligent and alert to where his eye leads him, he might fall into a ditch or even

drown in a creek. In the same way also the soul, which is clothed with the attractive garment—namely the body—possesses the ability to distinguish between good and evil and this acts as an eye to direct the soul, together with the body, as it passes through the scum and the thorns of this life, that is, the lusts and pleasures of this world. The soul should also wrap around itself vigilance, diligence, courage, attentiveness, and self-control, so that it will not be torn by thorns in the woods of this world, which represent anxieties, fears, bodily lusts, worldly cares and earthly worries" (Homily 4).

He adds that only through the anointing of the Holy Spirit will our eyes be opened to see God's way:
"Just as eyes that are open can clearly see the sun, so can the mind that has been fully sanctified see the glory of Christ openly and unite with Him, day and night, in the same way that the Body of Christ unites with the Holy Spirit" (Homily 17).

He goes on to affirm that we should aim to have our eyes illuminated by God so that we can see the way ahead,
"every enthusiastic trader works very hard in expectation of a profit. So also, in the kingdom of heaven, individuals put their lives fully in the Lord's hands, persevering in prayers and supplications, giving up all the lusts and desires of this world in the hope that God will illuminate the eyes of their hearts" (Homily 14).

The treasure of the Holy Spirit
For all the above reasons, Saint Macarius

demonstrates that the Holy Spirit is the real treasure that we must seek from God with unceasing seriousness. He says,

> "those who have the treasure of the Holy Spirit maintain the purity of their bodies and hearts with the simplicity of their eyes and thoughts, without any feeling of being deprived from any leisure of this world, nor any sense of struggle, as they are united with Him in all they do. Through this treasure they can easily fulfil all the fullness of righteousness and do all the commandments of the Lord without hardship. They keep simple eyes, pure hearts, clean bodies and heavenly thoughts without much struggle, as they have it all in that treasure given to them in the Holy Spirit, who continuously takes from Jesus and gives them according to their need in due time" (Homily 18).

Homily 50 shows that those who have access to this unlimited treasure while they are still weak and unworthy join together as a holy nation. These holy people join Saint Paul in saying "we have this treasure in earthen vessels, that the excellence of the power may be of God and not of us." Saint Macarius stresses that we must focus all our efforts and our attention on gaining this wonderful treasure of gifts and power:

> "each one of us must examine whether or not we have found the "treasure in earthen vessels" (2 Cor 4:7), and whether we have put on the royal robe of the Holy Spirit, seen the King of Kings and found rest by becoming closer to Him. If not, perhaps we still serve in the most exterior parts of the house" (Homily 50).

The word of God guides us to the truth
Saint Macarius explains that "the word of God is not idle; it has its own effective work on the soul." Therefore, he highlights the effect that the word of God has on us when we obey Him and submit to Him. He explains,
> "those who hear the word of God should take note of the work of the word in their own souls... For this reason, it is called a work, so that its effect may be found in those who hear it."

He adds,
> "for just as the shadow precedes the body, but reveals it, so also, while the truth is the body itself, the word is like a shadow of the truth of Christ. Thus, the word precedes the truth; accepting the word of God comes first, then Christ dwells in our hearts in truth" (Homily 30).

So, it is through submitting ourselves to the word of God that we come to know the truth inside ourselves. Therefore, he encourages us to take the word of God very seriously, immerse ourselves in it and accept it as it comes to us, and never neglect it or take it lightly;
> "God, the true King, has sent His divine scriptures to people as letters, pointing out to them that they need to call out to God, and, believing, they need to ask and to receive a heavenly gift from God the Holy Trinity Himself. For it is written; 'that through these you may be partakers of the divine nature' (2 Pet 1:4). But if a person does not approach and seek and receive, it will not benefit him or her to read the scriptures. But rather he or she is under the sentence of death, because he or she did not wish to receive the gift of life from the

heavenly King, without which it is impossible to obtain immortal life, which is Christ" (Homily 39).

The Sun of Righteousness

Saint Macarius seems to be fully aware of the deep-seated sin and weakness inside our souls:

"After the fall of Adam, the soil of the human heart produced thistles and thorns. Though a person takes pain to tend the soil frequently, the thorns of evil spirits still spring up, until the Holy Spirit Himself 'helps in our weaknesses (Rom 8:26) and the Lord plants heavenly seed in the soil of the heart and cultivates it. Though the holy seed has fallen into the soil, thistles and thorns still spring up. Only when the Lord Himself expertly tills the soil of the soul with His abundant grace, then the thistles dry up by the heat of the Sun of Righteousness (Mal 4:2)" (Homily 26).

He also adds,
"the souls of men are like a land full of muddy puddles but when the sun shines, it warms it up and turns it into dry clean land. Similarly, when the Sun of Righteousness shines on the children of God to heal them, they are filled with the Holy Spirit who takes away all their bad desires and makes them rich in grace" (Homily 16).

He contemplates on the way Malachi describes the effect of the Holy Spirit when he says "the Sun of Righteousness shall arise with healing in His wings; and you shall go out and grow fat like stall-fed calves" (Mal 4:2), then he sees that this change can only come from the Holy Spirit dwelling in us. Therefore, he teaches us that we need to persevere in our prayers, asking to be filled with the Holy Spirit in order to be completely healed from all our wounds and weaknesses,

> "brave people continue to cry out to God in a way that demonstrates the strength of their will and the honesty of their desire for God. Then the Sun of Righteousness, Jesus, shines gloriously in their hearts and His rays penetrate all their members and the greatest peace reigns in power in them" (Homily 16).

This very much echoes what Saint Paul advised his disciple Timothy:

> "but you, O man of God, flee these things and pursue righteousness, godliness, faith, love, patience, gentleness. Fight the good fight of faith, lay hold on eternal life, to which you were also called and have confessed the good confession in the presence of many witnesses" (1 Tim 6:11-12).

Christianity is food and drink

Saint Macarius feels that we must experience God and have a very close and dependent relationship with Him, like the one we have with food and drink. He strongly asserts that only talking about God or rehearsing some Biblical verses and spiritual phrases will never be enough to know Him. We need to experience Him as the food we eat and the water we drink. He likens those who talk about God without first-hand experience to someone who describes the honey he has never tasted to people who have never seen it. He adds,

> "those who talk about the spiritual life without personally experiencing it, are like a poor man who sees himself in a dream as a very rich man but he wakes up only to find out that he is still the

same poor man" (Homily 17).

He makes a very strong statement which is full of truth:

> "in fact, Christianity is food and drink!! The more you eat from it, the more you love it and your heart longs for it more as you continue eating from it and never feel full" (Homily 17).

Therefore, he frequently stresses that we only know Christ through true experiences with Him that open our eyes to His mystery as he says,

> "Christianity is not just a religion, it is a mystery and those who truly live in it always say 'this is a great mystery' (Eph 5:32). But the mystery of Christianity is alien to this world" (Homily 27).

We choose our destination by our free will

Saint Macarius regularly emphasizes the role of free will in choosing our destination, benefitting from the mercy of God, proving our love to Him and separating us from all the rest of the creation. He teaches:

> "God's grace and the enemy's evil power can dwell in the same heart side by side and work against each other to gain influence." And; "both sin and grace can try, at the same time, to influence the same heart" (Homily 17).

Therefore, he sees our free will as the discerning tool that shows our real desire and willful choices which count in front of God.

Saint Macarius explains that grace and sin are side by side for us to choose "sin and grace can dwell together in the same heart without any change in the nature of the grace of God" (Homily 16); so as he teaches, "the fact that war comes upon you is not your doing, however, it is up to you to hate it and to reject evil desires. Then the Lord, seeing the determination of your mind, that you are struggling and that you love Him with your whole soul, drives death away from your soul and receives you in His arms, into His light. In a flash, God snatches you from the jaws of darkness and immediately takes you into His kingdom. For God, all things are easily accomplished, if only you willingly show your love for Him. God wants to see peoples' free will at work, since the human soul is meant to have fellowship with the Holy Trinity" (Homily 26).

Moreover, he contrasts those who utilize their free will to resist evil thoughts against those who do not:
"Those who have accepted the partnership of sin by their own choice have given away their will to evil as they have made peace with Satan and stopped resisting him. But those who experience thoughts of sin that they have not chosen, and then do not consent to those thoughts, or take pleasure in them, or surrender to them, but oppose them in words and deeds, are far more noble and honorable in God's eyes than those who freely give their will over to the devil" (Homily 27).

He adds,
"by this transgression he was lost and was wounded. Though Satan darkened his mind, mankind was still alive, possessing a will that can differentiate good from evil" (Homily 26).

Therefore, he explains that in our journey on this Earth we continuously make many small daily decisions and also decide on big standpoints which are important steps on the way towards God:

> "The word of God, working in us, encourages us all to make our own willful decision to loosen ourselves from this earthly bond. This decision has to be made by our own free will because through our own free will we were bound by this earthly bond" (Homily 21).

He clearly believes in the harmony between our free will and the work of the Holy Spirit:

> "The Holy Spirit works with our soul in a mystical way while the individual patiently uses the opportunities that come his or her way to prove that he or she truly desires God. The grace of God works perfectly in those who have demonstrated over time that they have freely chosen to please the Holy Spirit by putting aside all world's passing pleasures and false promises" (Homily 9).

He even warns us about being complacent after accepting God's grace, as the free will that we each have needs to continue making those critical decisions throughout the journey of life:

> "Some people think that the soul, after receiving grace has no weakness, but in fact, God requires a person's free will to allow both the soul and the Holy Spirit to work together in full harmony" (Homily 17).

As we each continue to use free will to determine our directions, "eventually the soul belongs to the power it chooses; either God or Satan" (Homily 26), for "the mind goes where it finds its goal and the soul follows its love" (Homily 26).

True Christian or fake Christians

One of the main concepts which Saint Macarius introduces in his homilies is that there are two kinds of Christians; true Christians and fake Christians. He defines true Christians like this:

> "Christians are not of this world; they are children of the heavenly Adam, a new race, children of the Holy Spirit, shining brothers of Christ, similar to their Father, the spiritual Adam. Therefore, they belong to His city, His race and have His power. The Lord Himself says; 'You are not of this world, even as I am not of this world' (John 17:16)" (Homily 16).

He explains that generally, no ordinary person can differentiate between the two groups as there is no apparent difference in their external behavior, mannerisms, choice of words or clothes. But they are a world apart in their hidden life that is entirely united with the Holy Spirit as they reject all darkness of flesh and spirit, relying on God alone in order to be transformed into His image;

> "Those who have not been born of the Spirit from above (Jn 3:3) and are not true Christians, but only take on the external appearance of the true Christians through empty words, false humility and meaningless rituals are like those Jesus found unworthy to attend His Heavenly wedding" (Homily 4).

Moreover, the effect of Christianity only takes place in true Christians, as they live in and with Christ, who dwells in them, changing them into His image:

"Great and indescribable are the promises held out to true Christians. They are so great, indeed, that all the glory and beauty of heaven and earth cannot measure up to the beauty and riches of a single Christian soul" (Homily 4).

He explains that:
"True Christians have a whole world of difference between them and all other people [...] the rest of the world is one thing and they are another. The children of this world are like wheat in a sieve that is sifted by restless thoughts and the uncertainty of this world. They are constantly tossed to and fro by earthly cares, desires, and their love of material things. Satan tosses such souls as a sifter sifts wheat. Ever since Adam fell, by disobeying God's commandment, and came under the power of darkness, Satan has sifted the whole sinful human race using earthly cares, deceitful thoughts and unjustified agitation. As the wheat in the sieve is continually shaken by the sifter, Satan dashes them relentlessly against the sieve of this earth with many earthly concerns, negative thoughts and anxieties to keep them in bondage to this world... Only those who have been reborn from above and have been transformed in mind and heart and moved to another world can escape him, saying, 'our citizenship is in Heaven' (Phil 3:20) [...] true Christians always have their hearts and minds focused on heavenly matters as Saint Paul clearly explained to us that, 'if then you were raised with

Christ, seek those things which are above, where Christ is, sitting at the right hand of God' (Col 3:1). Therefore, while they are still in this world, they look at all the goodness of eternal life as if looking in a mirror for they have received the Holy Spirit and His fellowship that works in them as they are reborn again from the Father. They have received the right to be the children of God in truth and power 'as many as received Him, to them He gave the right to become children of God, to those who believe in His name' (Jn 1:12). When they reach an appointed steady stage of freedom, peace and tranquility, Satan is no longer able to sift them with those evil waves of restless thoughts. Moreover, they are greater than the whole world for they only care for Christ and for the love of the Holy Spirit, as they have 'passed from death into life' (Jn 5:24). What distinguishes true Christians from other people is not their external appearance, their use of certain humble words or their style of life, but the true love that Christians have in their hearts for all people and the purity of the thoughts in their minds, as Christ has become the main focus of their lives. Sadly, some Christians are very much like the rest of the world in their hearts and minds. They undergo the same disturbing restlessness and instability of their thoughts. They lack faith and suffer from confusion, agitation, and fear as all other people do. They may differ somewhat externally or in their choice of words or their way of acting in certain situations, but in their hearts and minds, they are still shackled by earthly bonds, like the rest of the world. They do not have the divine rest and heavenly peace of the Holy Spirit in their hearts because they never earnestly asked God for it, nor did they ever believe that He would stoop down to grant them these wonderful heavenly gifts" (Homily 5).

We ought to believe that God can and will free us from those shackles that are holding us back for He said, "if the Son makes you free, you shall be free indeed" (Jn 8:36).

He clearly rejects any suggestion that the external appearance is valuable, putting all his emphasis on the importance of the work of the Holy Spirit on the inner person.

"Some people are considered Christians by others merely because they have the outward appearance of righteousness. But, only those who bear the sign and image of the King, Jesus Christ, are true Christians. The rest are fake Christians and bogus workers who imitate the work of real Christians [...] true Christians and fake ones can look very similar in their external appearance and behavior, to the extent that they could deceive many people. Only experienced spiritual people can differentiate between the two" (Homily 38).

For this reason, he likens the difference between genuine and fake Christians to the difference between genuine and fake coins:

"Just as in the case of the golden coin, if it does not receive the imprint of the king's image, it is not considered genuine and so will neither reach the marketplace nor to be stored up in the royal treasuries, but will be discarded as fake. Similarly, if the soul does not have the image of the Holy Spirit stamped on it in indescribable light, it is not useful for the treasuries above and is cast out by the merchants of the kingdom, the Apostles" (Homily 30).

Our glorified bodies in resurrection
Saint Macarius gives us a very detailed vision of the state of our bodies in the resurrection in an amazing way that encourages us to seek the promised resurrection (Rev 7:9-17). He tells us that we will be covered with the glory of the Holy Spirit that has been dwelling in us during our life:

> "In the day of resurrection, by the power of 'the Sun of Righteousness' (Mal 4:2), the glory of the Holy Spirit will rise up from within, covering the bodies of true Christians to reveal the glory that they had treasured inside their souls during their lives on earth. This is the day in which their bodies will be glorified by means of the light that is currently hidden inside them [...] for the divine Spirit, who they have been considered worthy to possess, will then bring about in them every beauty of radiance and heavenly splendor. So, we all now can say: 'our citizenship is in heaven, from which we also eagerly wait for the Savior, the Lord Jesus Christ, who will transform our lowly body that it may be conformed to His glorious body, according to the working by which He is able even to subdue all things to Himself' (Philippians 3:20-21)" (Homily 5).

He even likens our bodies in the resurrection to the body of Moses after he had seen a glimpse of God's glory:

> "Therefore, each one of us ought to believe and press on in our devotion to live a full and upright life. With much hope and endurance, we should

acquire the privilege of receiving that heavenly power and the glory of the Holy Spirit inside our souls, so that after our bodies are dissolved, we may receive that beauty which shall clothe and revive us as the apostle says 'if indeed, having being clothed we shall not be found naked' (2 Cor 5:3), and 'He shall bring to life our mortal bodies by His Spirit that dwells in us' (Rom 8:11). For the blessed Moses provided us with a certain example through the glory of the Spirit, which covered his countenance, upon which no one could gaze. This example reveals how in the resurrection of the just, the bodies of the saints will be glorified with a glory, which, even now, the souls of saintly and faithful people are deemed worthy to possess, in the inner man [...] they are already considered worthy to have the power of the Holy Spirit in their souls because of this they exceed all other people. Therefore, their bodies will also be worthy to receive eternal blessings in the resurrection. They will be permeated with the glory of the Holy Spirit that their souls in this life have already experienced" (Homily 5).

He emphasizes with certainty that the glory we will have at the resurrection must be stored inside us during our earthly life like seeds that have all their future characteristics and abilities inside them, which will burst forth gloriously at the time of the final resurrection (Homily 32).

Full confidence in God's promises but without complacency

Orthodoxy according to Saint Macarius strongly reassures all true Christians that they can have full confidence in God's promise of salvation through His work in us:

> "Therefore, all of us need to persevere to attain every virtue and to believe that we can now possess that promised eternal building in heaven as our permanent residence [...] they fully trust with no fear that when the earthly house of their bodies is destroyed by death, they will move on to the incorruptible heavenly house of the glory of the Holy Spirit who will restore their bodies to the glory of the resurrection, as Saint Paul explained to us; 'if the Spirit of Him who raised Jesus from the dead dwells in you, He who raised Christ from the dead will also give life to your mortal bodies through His Spirit who dwells in you' (Rom 8:11), 'that the life of Jesus also may be manifested in our mortal flesh' and, 'for we who are in this tent groan, being burdened, not because we want to be unclothed, but further clothed, that mortality may be swallowed up by life' (2 Cor 4:11, 5:4)" (Homily 5).

He stresses the need to obtain the Kingdom of God even before we reach heaven:

> "Those whose anointing comes from the true tree of life who is Jesus Christ Himself, are given the privilege of attaining a high spiritual level of life through their adoption by our Lord God [...] Though they are still in the world and have not yet received the fulfilment of the promises given to them by our Lord, they enter into the kingdom as if they were already crowned because of the guarantee they have been given. Therefore, while they are still in the body, they understand the abundance of spiritual freedom because they

have already tasted the sweetness of God's fatherhood and the effect of His power" (Homily 17).

But he does not believe that salvation is complete before we go to heaven, as he asks us to be careful and diligent till we reach heaven:

"Some people settle in the grace of God and fully rely on it till they become much stronger than sin as they enjoy the life of prayers and peace. However, they always should remain careful because at any time they could fall under the influence of evil thoughts and the trickery of sin. Once inexperienced people feel the work of the grace of God in them, they falsely believe that sin no longer exists in their life. On the other hand, those who understand well, never dare to deny the trickery of sin and the power of unclean thoughts despite the fact that they live in the grace of God. They know that even when they are living in grace, they are still tested by wicked and unclean thoughts. The apostle clearly warned us saying; 'be vigilant; because your adversary the devil walks about like a roaring lion, seeking whom he may devour' (1 Peter 5:8)" (Homily 17).

Our trials and tribulations are the only way to our victory in Christ

Saint Macarius had his own fiery trial when the son of the village chief fell in love with a young woman from his village and when the signs of pregnancy became evident, he advised her to say that it was Macarius who made her pregnant for he wished to protect himself and the reputation of his socially prominent family (see Chapter 1). But, Macarius looking unto Jesus, "the author and finisher of our faith, who for the joy that was set before Him endured the cross, despising the shame" (Heb 12:2), did not attempt to defend himself, but accepted the accusation in silence as his Lord did (Mt 27:12). He was praying to God throughout this trial, thanking Him for sharing the cross and asking Him to sustain his faith and patience until the woman confessed his innocence when her labor became exceedingly difficult. Interestingly, immediately after enduring his trial, and as he refused to accept the false glory of this world, he saw one of the Cherubim, full of eyes and with six wings, who reassured him of God's support and showed him the way to the Nitrian desert where he started his monastic life. This was the beginning of his fellowship with the Holy Spirit. This experience must have taught him the intimate relationship between endurance of trials and the fullness of the Holy Spirit. Therefore, he brings to our attention an interesting Biblical message that the fellowship with the Holy Spirit begins when a person rejects the world by enduring many trials:

> "The Holy Spirit works with our soul in a mystical way while the individual patiently uses the opportunities that come his or her way to prove that he or she truly desires God. The grace of God works perfectly in those who have demonstrated over time that they have freely chosen to please the Holy Spirit by putting aside all the world's passing pleasures and false promises. There are many examples of this in the Bible. Joseph rejected the opportunity to sin with his master's wife. Instead he accepted imprisonment and dishonor, then later he was found to be upright in the sight of God who made him a leader over the whole of Egypt (Gen 39-41). The same happened to David. Though God anointed him king by the

hand of Samuel the prophet, he was dreadfully afflicted and had to flee into the desert because of Saul's plots to kill him. Though he was the one who God anointed to be king, he suffered many afflictions. But, after he had patiently endured everything, placing all his trust in God alone, God's promise to him was finally fulfilled. The same also happened to Moses. God arranged for him to become the son of Pharaoh's daughter and to grow up as a leader 'in all the wisdom of the Egyptians' and to be "mighty in words and deeds' (Acts 7:22), but only when he rejected all of these things; 'choosing rather to suffer affliction with the people of God than to enjoy the passing pleasures of sin, esteeming the reproach of Christ greater riches than the treasures in Egypt' (Heb 11:25-26), then God made him a savior for his people and like a god for Pharaoh (Exod 7:1) [...] all these examples from the Holy Scripture show us that the power of the Holy Spirit (which is given to the faithful souls) comes with much endurance and patience in trials and in testing circumstances. Our free will is put to the test by all sorts of afflictions. And when we 'do not grieve the Holy Spirit of God' (Eph 4:30) in any way but work in harmony with the grace of God by keeping all God's commandments, then God considers us worthy to be freed from evil desires. Jesus said, 'therefore if the Son makes you free, you shall be free indeed' (John 8:36)" (Homily 9).

He repeats the same message in Homily 17 to stress the contemporary relationship between the filling of the Holy Spirit and the beginning of temptations as he explained:

"Immediately, after David was anointed, he had to face many troubles and so do we. But, remember that the Holy Spirit is also called the Comforter because He comforts us in all our tribulations [...] when the Jews were in charge of the priesthood, some were persecuted because of their perseverance in the truth such as Eleazar and the Maccabees. Also, now, after the cross and the tearing of the veil in the temple, some Christians are persecuted similarly. Troubles come to the true Christians to give them a chance to witness to the truth, but they must continue to be watchful so they do not fall" (Homily 17).

But he reassures us that during the trials God Himself supports the suffering souls:
"the Lord rides the soul and guides it with the Spirit, directing it as He sees fit [...] He is the leader of our entire existence and takes us to wherever He wishes in our journey to heaven [...] what a good and wonderful leader He is, who will make us worthy of the glory of the resurrection, after He has glorified us, in our current life on earth, through our relationship with the Holy Spirit" (Homily 1).

As "the scripture says, 'the hand of a man was underneath their wings on their four sides' (Ezekiel 1:8). This is why Christ is the one who carries the soul and still directs it on the way" (Homily 1).

He adds another reassurance to give us confidence in the outcome of our trials and tribulations which is that the Lord Himself places precise limits on our trials which Satan cannot exceed:

> "Just as the potter controls the oven temperature to achieve the best quality for his pots, and like the goldsmith who expertly wields fire to fashion the best jewelry, it follows that God limits the enemy's power much more than that. God knows what sort of vessels humans are, so He only permits the enemy to have a limited measure of power. God knows how much each person is able to be a good steward, and gives him or her various gifts accordingly. That is clear in the book of Job, as Satan was unable to do anything by himself without permission from God [...] therefore, as far as a person seeks God's help and is eager to receive His grace, Satan desires to tempt him. In fact, he said to the Lord, 'does Job fear God for nothing? Have You not made a hedge around him, around his household, and around all that he has on every side? You have blessed the work of his hands, and his possessions have increased in the land. But now, stretch out Your hand and touch all that he has, and he will surely curse You to Your face' (Job 1:9-11)!" (Homily 26).

Saint Macarius likened the effect of trials to the effect of fire that fashions precious metals. He even explained the reason why some of the trials last longer than we sometimes wish:

> "Iron, gold or silver melts when thrown into the fire and is transformed from its hard nature to a soft substance as long as it remains in the fire. The same is true for the soul that receives that heavenly fire of the Holy Spirit; it is then truly freed from all attachments to the world and liberated from every evil affection. For 'the Lord

is the Spirit; and where the Spirit of the Lord is, there is liberty' (2 Cor 3:17). As the soul rejects the lusts and desires of this world, all its natural harsh characteristics change by the love of the heavenly bridegroom to the sweetness and gentleness of Him who died for it" (Homily 4).

Moreover, Saint Macarius considers trials essential for Christians to be filled with the Holy Spirit:
"Christians possess a glory and indescribable heavenly richness that come to them as a result of hard work and endurance in times of temptations and through many trials. All of this can only be attained by the grace of the Holy Spirit [...] they have tasted another unutterable beauty and have participated in other riches. They have received in the inner person another Spirit that is the Holy Spirit (Homily 5).

Therefore, Saint Macarius makes it very clear that:
"The faithful soul cannot attain all of this grace without many tribulations and trials. Through various trials, suffering and tribulations, the soul grows in grace and attains fellowship with the Holy Spirit. When a person endures all the evil trials with courage and patience, the soul reaches a full, fearless state and qualifies for all heavenly honor and spiritual gifts. 'Blessed is the man who endures temptation; for when he has been approved, he will receive the crown of life which the Lord has promised to those who love Him' (Jm 1:12). True Christians know that 'we must through many tribulations enter the kingdom of God' (Acts 14:22). But they always encourage

themselves saying, 'who shall separate us from the love of Christ? Shall tribulation, or distress, or persecution, or famine, or nakedness, or peril, or sword?' (Rom 8:35). This is the way we become heirs of the kingdom of our Lord Jesus Christ" (Homily 10).

He links our suffering to the Lord's suffering in a very encouraging way:
"All the righteous people had to go through many tribulations in their journey on the narrow road. Moreover, the Lord Himself suffered many tribulations and lived on this earth as though He had forgotten His divine glory, making Himself an example for us to imitate, 'but when you do good and suffer, if you take it patiently, this is commendable before God. For to this you were called, because Christ also suffered for us, leaving us an example, that you should follow His steps' (1 Pet 2:20-21). The apostles indeed followed the example of Christ in his suffering, therefore the Apostle also says through the Holy Spirit 'imitate me, just as I also imitate Christ' (1 Cor 11:1) [...] you should be crucified with Him who was crucified for you and suffer with Him who suffered for you, so that you can be glorified with Him who is always glorified. 'I have been crucified with Christ; it is no longer I who live, but Christ lives in me; and the life which I now live in the flesh I live by faith in the Son of God, who loved me and gave Himself for me' (Gal 2:20). There is no possible way except the narrow road of suffering by which we can enter the city of the saints where we find our rest and reign there with the King of kings forever and ever. This is

why Saint Peter advised us saying, 'beloved, do not think it strange concerning the fiery trial which is to try you, as though some strange thing happened to you; but rejoice to the extent that you partake of Christ's sufferings, that when His glory is revealed, you may also be glad with exceeding joy' (1 Pet 4:12-13). 'Therefore, since Christ suffered for us in the flesh, arm yourselves also with the same mind' (1 Pet 4:1)" (Homily 12).

Therefore, Saint Macarius believed that Christians do not reach this deep spiritual experience with God, where there is full freedom from their earthly bonds, until they have gone through many different trials and fiery difficulties;

"People do not reach that spiritual level in a moment but only after many trials, rejection of temptation and much labor in their journey with God that begins now and never ends as they are 'being transformed into the same image from glory to glory, just as by the Spirit of the Lord' (2 Cor 3:18)" (Homily 17).

He tells us:
"the Christians who have been found worthy and who press on for the perfect life in unity with Christ, dedicate themselves always to the cross of Christ as the Lord said, 'if anyone desires to come after Me, let him deny himself, and take up his cross, and follow Me' (Mt 16:24). As people are captured by the love of Christ, they are taken into a deep experience of God and are crucified with Him and sanctified in Him. In this way, they become children of God and are fully united with Him (Homily 17).

He explains the value of the cross in the process of transforming us to the image of His Son:

"The Holy Spirit works with us like men working with wild horses to tame them. Wild horses are not useful to people if they are not tamed. For them to become reasonable and beneficial, men work patiently and consistently with them to train them to accept a new way of living. Likewise, the Holy Spirit patiently and consistently works with us, in our minds and hearts, to make us useful members of the royal family of God and citizens of heaven" (Homily 23).

Then after these souls are tamed, Jesus,
"arms them with the breastplate of righteousness, the helmet of salvation, the shield of faith, and the sword of the Spirit (Eph 6:14-17). Then those souls are taught to wage a spiritual war against the real enemies "to quench all the fiery darts of the wicked one" (Eph 6:16). As the faithful souls obtain those spiritual weapons of the Holy Spirit, they experience severe wars and sufferings, but only by crying out to the Lord they defeat the enemies. And so, having fought the war and shared in the victory with the help of the Holy Spirit, the soul receives crowns of victory with great glory" (Homily 23).

"Indeed it was for my own peace that I had great bitterness; but You have lovingly delivered my soul from the pit of corruption, for You have cast all my sins behind Your back" (Is 38:17).

He explains the purpose behind the trials:

"Indeed, our free choice is tested by situations designed to help us to grow and progress in our journey towards Him. These situations show whether a person is continually united with the grace of God, until he or she gradually fully comes to be one with the Spirit. Then, he or she becomes holy and pure by the work of the Holy Spirit, and thus is made fit for the Kingdom of Heaven" (Homily 24).

He advises us to be patient at times of troubles and trials:
"the ones who have a strong and deep relationship with the Holy Spirit and are rich in grace, know how to wait for the mercy of God in difficult times, when they do not feel God's support. Therefore, in times of trouble they do not fall into despair. They call on God who certainly supports them, for He fully understands their needs and knows their thoughts" (Homily 16).

He stresses the same advice in a different way:
"Occasionally while a person is comforted in his journey with God, God could withdraw His grace from him or her and he or she could be delivered up to temptations. The devil comes, bringing multiple waves of negative feelings, experiences and thoughts such as despair, pain, troubles, fears and evil thoughts in an attempt to weaken the soul in order to alienate it from God so that it no longer hopes. Nevertheless, the prudent person does not give up hope, instead he or she holds onto the promises of God and as much as the devil brings against him or her, he or she endures in the face of all dangers and temptations, saying even if

I die, I shall not let him go (Song 3:4). Then, if a person endures faithfully to the end, the Lord begins to converse with Satan saying, "you see how many evils and afflictions you have inflicted upon him and yet he has not obeyed you, but he continues to serve Me and fear Me." Satan is then overcome by shame and has nothing further to say. In the case of Job, if the devil had known that Job would remain faithful despite temptation and would not be conquered, he would certainly never have desired to try to make him fall, out of fear of being humiliated. So also, now, in the case of those who bear afflictions and temptations, Satan is put to shame as he has attained nothing" (Homily 26).

He warns us that Satan does not stop waring against us but we should not fear any harm:

"Satan never gives up in his fight against us. As long as a person lives in the flesh in this world, he or she is subject to Satan's wars. However, when 'the fiery darts of the wicked one are quenched' (Eph 6:16), he can inflict no harm on people. If someone manages to become such a close friend of the king that no one from the king's ranks of nobles dares to prevent him from reaching the king, then no adversary can stand against him. So also, true Christians who live in unity with God as partakers of the divine nature (2 Pet 1:4), fear no harm, even if they are attacked in war by Satan, as they are not only friends with God but also united with Him" (Homily 26).

But peace in times of trouble comes only from the Holy Spirit:

"Just as the Lord put on a human body, leaving behind every heavenly principality and power, in a similar way Christians should also put on the Holy Spirit in order to find peace. Even if war starts externally as Satan attacks, they are still fortified internally by the Lord's power. Therefore, they are not anxious or worried about Satan. When Satan tempted the Lord in the wilderness for forty days, no harm came to Him. Although Satan attacked His body externally, he could do nothing to Him internally as He was God. So we Christians, may be tempted externally by Satan, nevertheless, internally we are filled with the Holy Trinity, therefore we suffer no harm. If someone has reached this level of spirituality, he or she has experienced the perfect love of Christ and the fullness of the Divine nature of God. But a person who is not at this level still struggles with interior wars, because at certain times he or she delights in prayer, but at other times he or she is bombarded by the afflictions of war. Since such a person is still an infant, the Lord trains him or her in war like a father trains his own son to defend himself [...] unless he or she is strengthened in the Lord, Satan will always try to overthrow him or her. This is how many who have been given grace went astray and lost that grace because they thought that they had obtained perfection while they were still far from it" (Homily 26).

Saint Macarius believes that as He suffered for us, we ought to suffer for Him:
"If even Jesus appeared outwardly poor and was humiliated like one of us, we should not ever despise His Divine glory, because for our sakes

He appeared on earth in a common, simple human body. Consider how He was humiliated more than all men at the hour when the crowd gathered against Him and cried out, 'crucify Him, crucify Him' (Lk 23:21). And what more humiliation could He have undergone after they spat in His face and placed a crown of thorns on Him and slapped Him? For it is written that, 'I gave My back to those who struck Me, and My cheeks to those who plucked out the beard; I did not hide My face from shame and spitting' (Is 50:6). If God accepts such insults and sufferings and humiliation, we, who by nature are made of earthly matter and are mortal, will never experience anything similar to our Lord no matter how much we are humiliated. God humbled Himself for our sake, so how can we refuse to be humbled for our own sakes? However, most of the time, we remain self-centered, proud and inflated. He came to take our afflictions and sufferings on Himself and to grant us His rest. Yet we often refuse to bear any difficulties or suffering that will result in the healing of our wounds" (Homily 26).

He equally reminds us of the glory waiting for us in heaven when we endure temptations:

"As Jesus sat at the right hand of the Father after He suffered on the cross and was glorified (Acts 2:33), so it is also necessary for you to suffer with Him, to be crucified with Him, and thus to ascend to be seated with Him at the right hand of the Father as being joined to the Body of Christ" (Homily 27).

"As 'indeed we suffer with Him, that we may also

be glorified together (Rom 8:17) [...] but He also allows grace to discipline and guide you. And when you reach this state of rest and surrender, grace makes you understand the path of your training and its advantages for your soul. It is like a rich man who sends his child to a tutor. For a while the tutor disciplines him in a way that seems harsh, until the child becomes an adult. Then he begins to be grateful to his tutor. God, also, in His prudence and love, chooses grace to discipline you until you become fully mature" (Homily 32).

He believes that one of the main reasons we fall from grace and fail to reach a state of maturity and rest with God is because we do not bear the cross in times of trouble:

"many simple people who receive grace are like little cities fortified by the power of Christ. They only fall away from grace for two reasons:
1) either because they do not persevere patiently in bearing the afflictions brought to them, or 2) because they have tasted the pleasures of sin and continued in them. Those who journey towards God cannot reach their goal without many trials. When giving birth, a beggar and a queen both have the same sufferings, so likewise neither the land of a rich man, nor the land of a poor man can produce worthy fruit unless the land is toiled. So too in the working of the soul, neither the wise man nor the rich man grows in grace, unless it is through patience and many labors. Every time you face trouble remember that the Spirit says 'for indeed I am for you, and I will turn to you, and you shall be tilled and sown' (Ezk 36:9)" (Homily

42).

He clearly sees the cross as an essential step before being filled with the Holy Spirit. He uses the example of the burnt sacrifice that had to be slaughtered first and then seasoned with salt before it could be offered to Christ as a sacrifice:

> "In the Law of Moses, God commanded that the priest should first kill every sacrifice, then season it with salt before placing it on the fire. This is to say that unless the priest first kills the lamb, it will not be salted nor will it be brought to the Lord as a burnt offering. In the same manner, our souls must come to Christ, our High Priest, to be slain by Him and die to the world and to sin, for the life of wicked passions must be expelled out of the soul (Homily 1)."

Saint Macarius strongly advises us to force ourselves to fully trust God in times of trouble as the gospel says "let those who suffer according to the will of God commit their souls *to* Him in doing good, as to a faithful Creator" (1 Pet 4:19).

Therefore, he adds:

> "For as every one of us forces and compels himself or herself to pray despite the reluctance of his or her own heart, we should also force ourselves to trust God" (Homily 19).

Conclusion

We are now sure that without Him we can do nothing (Jn 15:5) and we always need the Holy Spirit to give us life (Jn 6:63). Saint Macarius summarizes his teaching by saying:

"God was pleased to come down from the holy heavens and take on Himself your physical nature. He took flesh from the earth and joined it with His Divine Spirit, so that you, who are from the earth, might receive a heavenly soul. When your soul has fellowship with the Holy Spirit, and His heavenly soul enters your soul, you are a perfect person in God, and an heir and son of God [...] as you begin to fight the war between your desire to follow God and your old nature, you pit thoughts against thoughts, mind against mind, soul against soul, spirit against spirit, and your soul experiences agony [...] the Lord who is near to your soul and your body sees your battle and gives you power and puts heavenly thoughts inside you as He begins to give you rest internally" (Homily 32).

Let us ask the Lord to draw near to our souls and our bodies to give all of us His power and to put His heavenly thoughts inside us so that we reach His eternal rest as victorious soldiers and glorified children whose "God is not ashamed to be called their God" (Heb 11:16).

May our loving Lord,

"who has saved us and called us with a holy calling, not according to our works, but according to His own purpose and grace which was given to us in Christ Jesus before time began, but has now been revealed by the appearing of our Savior Jesus Christ, who has abolished death and brought life and immortality to light through the gospel" (2 Tim 1:9-11)

guide us to His Kingdom through "the communion of the Holy Spirit" (2 Cor 13:14). Amen.

Bibliography

Aegyptius, Macarius, and Arthur James Mason. *Fifty Spiritual Homilies of St. Macarius the Egyptian*. London: Soc. f. prom. Christ. Knowl., 1921.

Al-'Māl al-Kmālah lil-Qdīs Ānbā Maqār: Al-'Żāt al-Khmsūn. Complied by Br. Younan al-Makary. Edited by Fr. Yohanna al-Makary and Fr. Wadeed al-Makary. Cairo: Saint Macarius Monastery Press, 2017

Al-Miskin, Matta. *Sīr al-Thalāt Maqarāt al-Qdisīn*. Cairo: Monastery of the Syrians, 1968.

Al-Miskin, Matta. *Sīrat al-Qdīs Maqarīus al-Kbīr*. Cairo: Monastery of the Syrians, 1968.

Beck, Aaron T. *Cognitive Therapy of Depression*. New York: Guilford Press, 2003.

Epiphanius, Bishop. *Bustān al-Rohbān*. Cairo: St. Macarius Monastery Press, 2013.

Malaty, Tadros. *'Izāt al-Qdīs Maqāriūs al-Kbīr*. Cairo: St. George Coptic Orthodox Church Sporting.

Marriott, George L. "The Messalians; and the Discovery of Their Ascetic Book." *Harvard Theological Review* 19, no. 2 (1926): 191–98. https://doi.org/10.1017/s0017816000007677.

Pseudo-Macarius. *The Fifty Spiritual Homilies and The Great Letter*. Edited and translated by George A. Maloney. New York: Paulist Press, 1992.

Tharwat, Maher Naguib. "Characteristics of Christian Piety: A Conversation between the Eastern Desert Fathers' Tradition and the Wesleyan Tradition Concerning the Aim of Christian Life," 2010.

Youhannes, Bishop. *Bustān al-Roh*. Cairo: St. Roweis Press, 1981.

Villecourt, L. 'La Grande Lettre Grecque de Macaire. Ses formes textuelles et son milieu litttraire,' *Revue de l'Orient Chretien*, (1920).

About the Author

George Tadros was born in Alexandria, Egypt, the Pearl of the Mediterranean. Like many young Copts, he was ordained to the diaconate as a reader (Anaghnostos) in 1973 by the late Bishop Bishoy, Secretary General of the Coptic Holy Synod. He moved to the United Kingdom in 1995 where he was ordained by Bishop Missael of Birmingham and Midlands as sub-deacon (Epideacon) in 2000 and Deacon in 2016. He served in Sunday School ministry in Egypt and the United Kingdom. He is married and had two daughters whom he loves dearly.

He graduated from Alexandria Medical School in 1986 (MB BCh), and specialized in Psychiatry and Neurology in 1993 (PG Dip). He became a member of the Royal College of Psychiatrists, London, (MRCPsych) in 1998 and fellow (FRCPsych) in 2016. He earned his Doctorate of Medicine (MD) from Keele University (England) in 2004. He is currently a Consultant Psychiatrist and Professor of Psychiatry and Dementia in Aston Medical School (United Kingdom) and adjunct professor of Psychiatry in Cairo Medical School (Egypt).

He believes that patristic teachings and texts serve as well-established roadmaps for subsequent generations, across the world and from all cultures, to march confidently into the future, shadowed by the Grace of God.

www.ingramcontent.com/pod-product-compliance
Lightning Source LLC
Chambersburg PA
CBHW030513080526
44586CB00011B/178